SHRM CP & SCP Exam Prep 2019-2020

A 2-in-1 Study Guide with 640 Test Questions and Answers for the Society for Human Resource Management Tests

Table of Contents

Introduction

Thank you for taking a look at this study guide for the SHRM-CP and SCP tests. These are tests that are critical to analyzing your ability to manage the functions pertaining to human relations. It is a necessity for anyone who is interested in entering the HR field to receive proper certification.

This guide includes a full review of the individual segments you will work with when faced with the SHRM-CP and SCP tests. These include the SHRM Body of Competency and Knowledge. The segments entail the behavioral functions you are expected to know and your technical ability. From leadership and navigation to communication to strategies, you will find everything that you need to understand throughout this guide.

There are four exams in this guide that simulate the test that you would take for HR certification. These include two separate exams for the SHRM-CP test and two for the SHRM-SCP test. The CP test is for those who are entering the human relations field, while the SCP test is designed mainly for those who have experience with the test and need to complete certain tasks.

Chapter 1 – The Exams

The SHRM-CP and SCP exams are both critical for those who have a strong interest in entering the human resources field. The Society for Human Resource Management established the Certified and Senior Certified Professional exams to gage the ability of people to handle various functions of human resources. You will have to understand the factual details surrounding the exam and how well you can complete tasks. You must also notice the situations that you might encounter.

The SHRM tests have 160 multiple choice questions; 95 of these questions are general knowledge; the other 65 questions are situational questions. You will be given a hypothetical situation and four answers to choose from.

The Certified Professional or SHRM-CP segment is for those who have been in the HR field for a brief period. A person who has an HR-related Bachelor's Degree needs one year of experience in an HR role to qualify for the exam. A person with a non-HR degree would need two years of experience. People with less than a Bachelor's Degree need three to four years of experience in the HR field in order to qualify to take the test.

The Senior Certified Professional or SHRM-SCP test focuses on advanced concepts of HR. You would be able to complete the SCP test three years after successfully completing the CP test. You are required to have a Bachelor's Degree in an HR field and to have spent at least four years in an HR role to quality to write the SCP test.

Body of Knowledge

The subject matter of the SHRM-CP and SCP exams are based on the SHRM Body of Competency and Knowledge information. This is the body of knowledge that covers five critical segments.

1. Behavioral Competencies

The behavioral competency segment has questions surrounding leadership skills, your business acumen, and how well you can handle relationships. Points on ethics and critical evaluation and consultation and communication skills as well are included. SHRM exams also include global and cultural awareness.

2. People

This segment entails an analysis of how you work with the people. You will need to review how you find and hire people and also understanding how you're going to engage with those people. You may also find questions surrounding how to reward the workers in your environment.

3. Organization

Organizational questions focus on employees and how to manage them after they join your group. This includes how you relate to your workers. Legal details of HR and technology are also covered in this section.

4. Workplace

The workplace segment involves understanding how you will manage risks relating to employment law. Corporate social responsibility is also covered. (Note: The aspects relating to employment law and regulations are only relevant to those who are testing within the United States. The details are critical for understanding the legal aspects of working.)

5. Strategy

The strategies can entail anything surrounding the different tasks that are involved in HR. These strategies will offer suggestions for planning activities within the daily routines in HR.

About a third of the questions in the CP exam and about half of the questions in the SCP exam focus on the behavioral aspects of working in HR.

Chapter 2 – Behavioral Competencies

The segment on behavioral competencies encompassing half the questions on the SHRM tests. There are eight behavioral competencies involved in this field of human resources.

This includes recognizing how well you are able to work with other people and promote a comfortable work environment. This section also includes understanding how to navigate and resolve the most difficult situations in the workplace.

Leadership and Navigation

Leadership and navigation is an aspect of behavioral competencies that entails understanding what can be done to be a better leader in the work environment. This includes establishing trust and how to motivate people to perform at their best.

General Goals

A person who wishes to be a better leader must be capable of navigating and understanding the organization and to express and promote the needs that a business holds. This includes reviewing the processes that are required within the business to keep it active.

What Makes a Good Leader?

James Kouzes and Barry Posner state that for a leader to be effective, that person needs to work with the following points for success:

1. The leader needs to be someone who has a good process in mind while also being willing to make the right changes. This includes knowing what is best for a business to thrive.

2. A shared vision has to be conveyed by the leader. The leader must know is appropriate and useful based on the goals of the company.

3. The leader must also be someone who knows how to encourage others to act. The key is to allow everyone to collaborate and be part of the solution.

4. A leader is a great model. The person does what is necessary for a project to be successful and has the ability to explain to others what makes certain tasks worthwhile and interesting.

5. A leader must be able to move beyond disappointments or adversity. A leader needs to encourage the people in the workplace to overcome problems they could experience in their work.

Five Essential Skills for Every Leader

A person who wants to be the best possible leader has to have the right skills for the task.

1. The leader has to be aware of the emotions people have and what concerns might cause actions to change.

2. Self-regulation is vital for keeping one's emotions and actions in check. A sense of control is necessary so as not to let emotions rule.

3. Every great leader is motivated and has a positive feeling toward the work.

4. Empathy is essential for harmony in the workplace. The leader should be able to give effective feedback with reasonable suggestions for improvement. They must be able to understand the worries of others in the workplace.

5. Social skills are also critical. How you communicate with others will affect the work that others produce.

The Inner Team

Erica Fox identifies four types of people essential for the inner team. The inner team sets the attitude of the entire workforce within the work environment to help others perform at their individual jobs so that they are more proficient and effective.

1. Inspirational Dreamer

The inspirational dreamer of the inner team has the vision for the team and what the goals of the team should be.

2. Analytical Thinker

An analytical thinker is a person who will have a better plan in mind and will use facts and logic in determining what is right. Risks and consequences should be analyzed. The analytical thinker will devise ways to make changes and what ideas might be useful for any project the inner team is planning.

3. Practical Warrior

A practical warrior is a person who has strong willpower that is necessary to stick with a plan. The proper actions must be taken while the truths are spoken regardless of what might be happening in the workplace. It is essential for the practical warrior to explain what one wants to do to the public even if whatever is being planned out is tough to convey or plan out.

4. Emotional Lover

The emotional lover is all about expressing one's feelings and hopes for others. The person will connect to others through emotions. This is to establish a feeling of trust among people. This can also facilitate general collaborative efforts.

Collaboration

Five steps must be followed to encourage a sense of collaboration within a group:

1. Understand the stakeholders in the situation. Look at the roles of the stakeholders to determine what is to be done and how those people are going to work with you.
2. Decide what is at stake in your work. Each task involved should have a goal. This includes recognizing the challenges or events in the workplace that will influence the goal.
3. Recognize the attitudes of the stakeholders about working toward the determined goal. Detailed plans are needed to allow everyone to work together.
4. Expectations for what is to be done have to be defined. You should also discuss specifics for the input of the stakeholders and how you're going to give feedback.

5. Respect the input and understand what makes certain things valuable to those workers. The people in question need to feel as though they are a part of the decision-making process.

Getting Tasks Done

You must plan the tasks that you're going to assign to the workforce. A leader must be ready to plan activities and make many things work within a group. This includes organizing resources and making sure all things that are necessary are available. The work process has to include the best ways to use resources.

A leader needs to be able to adapt to changes and to be innovative. This may include finding new ideas for how tasks are to be finished. The concept of leadership is different from being a manager. A manager will focus on trying to meet end goals and assigning someone to make sure those goals are met.

A vision must also be established. A leader's vision involves looking at a task and deciding what every person can do to get it completed. A vision allows people to be inspired. They will understand what they have to do if they're going to move forward and be more successful in the work they are doing.

A leader will understand that it is fine to fail so long as that person learns a lesson for what should be done in the future to resolve the problem in question.

Consensus Management

A leader needs to establish a consensus among all the people in the workplace. Consensus management entails getting people to agree on the direction of the business. The key is to see that the work in question meets the best interests of all people involved with the task. A sensible effort is made to allow any concerns that people have to be raised. Everyone involved with a particular task must be able to support the decision made by management regardless of whether or not that person feels positive or not.

Part of attaining consensus may entail finding persuasive ways to help people understand what makes certain strategies or plans beneficial. Some additional effort may help to make these ideas more appealing to the public. You must still be sensible in letting other people know why your ideas should be considered.

Transformational Efforts

A team must be supported by a transformational leader if it is to move forward. This means that a leader must have a sense of power over other people. A good vision and a sense of strategy are critical to success and for meeting goals.

Emotional intelligence is needed for one's success. Emotional intelligence is being able to recognize the perspectives of others. This includes looking at what drives the behaviors of other people who need to complete their tasks. The values of the organization should still be arranged well in this process. The leader should encourage other people in the workforce to complete tasks while allowing for positive changes to be made as necessary.

Essentials for Senior Professionals

Senior professionals will have to use a few additional considerations for leadership:

1. A person must be willing to develop others.

A senior professional must be ready to establish positive relationships with others and to develop the needs that people have. The values that those people have should be encouraged based on what you feel is appropriate in the workplace. In addition, the leader will help people understand many considerations surrounding what might be right for them to follow and where they are going to go into the work environment. Be aware of the needs of each person in your work environment when deciding what might work the best for someone's growth.

2. Changes should be planned.

Sometimes changes might have to be made. A senior leader has to communicate with people both what has to be done and why something needs to be completed. Proper collaboration is also necessary to allow people to accept the changes while explaining to everyone why some of these changes are critical. Part of this may also include communicating with others about what has to be done so that the business will grow and thrive.

A commitment is needed from the workforce. It is often difficult for people to change, but a quality leader will help others accept change as a challenge.

3. A senior leader is the voice of the HR department.

The HR department needs to be human. A leader should be ready to help employees and represent them in any situation. The leader has to be a champion for employees and respect the needs that those people have in the work environment.

4. There needs to be accountability.

A leader must see that everyone in the workforce is held accountable for their contribution to the projects being done properly and on time. Outcomes should be planned and those plans relayed to the workforce so they know what is expected.

5. The organizational culture in the workplace has to be planned.

The culture that a business promotes refers to the behaviors and values that influence the work being done in the workplace. New values must be accounted for to promote the best possible values for work.

6. The leader must also be able to convince the workforce to accept the necessary changes.

A leader should get people to buy into changes from the top down. The senior-most people in the workplace should first agree on the changes. Transparency is essential. Transparency is being direct with the people in the workplace and give logical reasons for the changes.

Input from others should be encouraged in the process of accepting change enthusiastically. To do this, the leader must be convincing and open to suggestions that are reasonable.

Things That a Leader Should not Do

You've read about the many things that a leader has to do to achieve success. Now it is time to look at what a leader should not do.

You must be careful about how you are winning, as winning at all costs may end up being a liability in the long run.

Avoid negativity if you intend to be an effective leader. You might need to help people change their actions and functions, but you need to ensure that you avoid being hostile or judgmental toward others.

Not listening to people or being overly judgmental can also become a threat to your work. You need to analyze what is right for your business and how you're going to move forward with your efforts. Anyone who refuses to take responsibility for certain actions or listen to people who should be supported will not gain the respect of the workforce.

Business Acumen

The business acumen refers to knowing how a business operates and knowing your competition. You can analyze the quality of your business and align your work based on what is right.

1. You'll need to know how to develop strong business relationships.

A good relationship is critical for your success when it comes to running a business. A strategic relationship is providing what the other business or entity needs. You will get what you require out of the process as well. Your relationships have to be planned with a strategy in mind based on who would help you the most and how well a group is going to assist you in any situation.

2. Review the general operational processes.

You'll have to plan a sensible routine for the business operations. The routine plans should be based on some of the actions that you're going to follow. The key is to see that there are no concerns about your plans for the business.

3. Review the quality of your industry.

You've got plenty of competition to deal with in your industry. You must observe how your competition operates. Look at how your industry is growing and thriving when compared with other businesses.

4. Organizational metrics must be used.

Organizational metrics are vital for helping you with your plans. Such metrics will analyze how well functions are working within your organization. You can also use metrics to make decisions about how to hire the right people for the appropriate jobs.

You can review the revenue or expenses for each employee you are working with. The revenue per employee is a measure of the revenue divided by the number of employees. This includes individual departments or your entire business in general. The measurements can be adapted to fit the goals you've established or how you want your business to move forward.

5. Technology can be utilized in your work environment.

An HR professional must be ready to leverage the technology that is available for the tasks at hand. The technology can be anything from new computers to mobile devices. Whether it entails communicating with people or planning new events, you'll need to see how well the technology you're using works to your benefit.

Senior Professionals

1. Analyze your risks.

Review the risks that your business may encounter. A senior HR professional should analyze how well risks are being handled based on various internal and external threats. There are four points that may be noticed:

- The strengths of a business involve what the group can handle. This includes things that can assist a business in developing leverage over others.

- Be aware of the weaknesses in your company. These can be any deficiencies that a company has including problems with providing the proper materials necessary for completing particular tasks.

- Opportunities can come from outside the business. Don't overlook opportunities that might be relevant to your business.

- The threats to your business need to be identified. These threats can come from outside your business or within and can be anything from economic worries to changes in the competition. These external threats can influence how well your business is capable of competing with others.

2. Review the strategies that you have established and compare them to your objectives.

Various things might change based on the strategy you want to use versus the changes that might occur. You can analyze your strategy based on as many financial or productivity standards that you want to incorporate in your work.

3. Review the solutions that you feel are appropriate.

You have to define your problems at the start, followed by identifying the options you have. You must also evaluate each of the options you have to work with based on what is sensible and logical for your business to follow. An appropriate option should be planned with an implementation that is sensible.

4. Prepare benchmarks for the competition.

The competition can be analyzed based on how the group is working. You'll have to discover what is making certain businesses more proficient and effective than yours. Determine what strategies other businesses are using that could be implemented in your workplace.

5. Review the economic factors that work in your field.

Many economic factors have to be considered. Part of this includes looking at employee benefits or other financial functions in your workplace and deciding how different concepts might work to your benefit.

6. You also have to consider how to influence government policies.

Governmental policies could be influenced in many ways depending on what you feel is sensible. You have the power to influence those in power to change rules based on what you feel is right for your plans for your company. Part of this includes looking at the guidelines for compliance and any laws that have to be followed.

7. Establish strategies for your business and work with different leaders within your industry.

You should talk with others within your industry to learn what other senior leaders are doing that you could implement to benefit your company.

Planning Your Business Acumen

Review your business acumen by:

1. State the problem as briefly as possible. Keep the problem statement to one paragraph if possible.

2. Review the project objectives you have set for your business. You can use up to seven points for your objectives if possible.

3. Identify the background of your company and factors should be identified based on budget, skills, and the competition of your business. Identify what is necessary to resolve the problems you've identified in the workplace.

4. Analyze any current processes you're working with. This is especially the case if you have external partners who might not understand what you are facing.

5. Detail the requirements you have for keeping your business operational. These requirements may include your staff members, and the assets that you need to acquire, the budget you have to work with, print materials, and technology and software necessary for your operation.

6. Determine some reasonable alternatives. Try to devise two or three alternatives to your plans. These may help you in cases where you've got concerns surrounding your initial plans.

7. Analyze the potential impact that might occur. You might also have to work with specific vendors or other partners depending on your plans.

8. You can also create specific action plans based on what you feel might work the best for your business. Action plans can be short-term objectives that will happen in the next few weeks or months or long-term plans for the future.

9. A one-page executive summary will explain to all concerned should be prepared. You must adjust your message to suit your audience. You should use a proposal based on the executive summary that explains where your business will go or what you feel might be right for the business.

Ethical Practice

You cannot afford to allow your behavior to be a concern. SHRM states that ethical considerations are personal and professional integrity. You must also be an ethical agent who is capable of getting people to follow the correct and ethical policies in order for a business to grow and thrive.

Anything that entails breaking these rules for how work is to be managed could be interpreted as being unethical.

Several points must be used when managing ethical ideas:

1. People have to maintain confidentiality.

Confidentiality refers to protecting the information of the company and of the employees. All HR professionals have to understand the need for confidentiality. This includes company details that might influence how a business operates.

2. A strong sense of integrity is required.

Integrity is critical to how well a business is to grow and function. The positivity that comes with the work in question should be planned while recognizing the efforts that have to be followed. People who recognize the integrity of the situation will feel increasingly confident in senior management and their decisions.

3. Anything unethical must be resolved immediately.

This includes making sure people within the company follow the correct rules in the workplace. The problems of unethical behavior have to be resolved as soon as they are identified. A formal investigation by law enforcement may be needed.

4. People should be encouraged to report unethical behaviors.

Anything unethical that is not reported may become a habit for some people, thus hampering the ability of the workforce and damaging the company. People should feel safe to report ethical concerns and unethical behavior.

5. Consistency in ethics is necessary.

Consistency is a critical aspect of getting the workplace to stay functional and within the law. Consistency means ensuring that all people, especially the leaders, understand what should be done when confronted with unethical behavior. There is no place for hypocrisy in the workplace.

6. Mistakes must be acknowledged.

Ethics states that people need to find ways to admit their mistakes and to take responsibility so they can commit to change in the future and to recover from these difficult mistakes. Much of this includes knowing how to correct the problems one has produced and how those issues can be resolved sooner. Those who are honest and direct about their mistakes will make it easier for others in the workplace to trust and support.

7. Bias must be avoided.

Bias is a significant problem that can directly influence how well business functions. You'll have to notice what people are assuming or thinking. Ethics requires looking at all the things that influence people's thoughts and actions and how they develop. It is critical for people to notice many considerations surrounding biases and to look at ways for those biases to be resolved and corrected.

8. All stakeholders must be heard.

All stakeholders in the workplace have value. These people need to discuss concepts about how they can contribute so that they feel comfortable and positive about what they are doing at work. The stakeholders will feel confident in their abilities if they are consulted.

Senior Professionals

Senior HR professionals will have to consider other concepts of ethics and how to use them:

1. Internal controls must be managed to ensure no conflicts of interest can develop in the work environment.

A conflict of interest can occur when one person considers their personal motives for gain and not the business. Proper controls have to be used to ensure there are no such conflicts involved in the work and the business.

2. A sense of contemporary understanding is critical.

There exists a need to look at one's understanding of various concepts that might become an issue. This includes looking at how certain ideas may be processed based on what new ideas or concepts are in the field of work. Having a contemporary sense of understanding also improves the credibility of the senior professional.

3. A senior HR professional has to handle the pressure of the operations of the business.

The pressures that one might experience in the workplace are often frustrating. However, it is through a senior professional's work that it becomes easy for a business to grow and thrive. A professional should recognize how these stresses can be handled successfully.

4. The senior leaders need to establish suitable policies for ethics.

The organization's success must be balanced with the ability to support the needs that employees have regarding how well they might work. Senior leaders have to be ready to establish the right policies without problems involved. New ethics policies have to be established surrounding what business members should be doing or how certain ideas have to work. The values that a business holds and what might be planned out in the work environment should be arranged well to where a business recognizes the suitable points it might need to follow.

5. All practices must be aligned with the goals of the company.

The HR efforts involved may include looking at employee training, recruiting or with motivational plans. Managers should also recognize the goals of the company and what might work the best in the work environment and how they are to be organized for success.

Relationship Management

Relationship management entails working with others by building the best possible relationships and by networking with others. Being able to negotiate deals with those people and to manage conflicts that may arise can dictate the overall success of a relationship.

Producing Credibility

A business has to show a sense of credibility. An HR person has to know how to handle the information quickly and then move forward with the right action. Failing to use the right data can be risky. It only takes one negative issue for a person's reputation to be significantly harmed. Therefore, a credible HR manager will work with all the technical competencies that one has while expressing those values as effectively as possible.

Respect must be given to the people in the workplace. The HR professional must understand the needs that others have. This includes looking at the ways that other people want to live their lives. People who are treated with respect will be more likely to respect an HR professional's words.

Establishing Better Relationships by Listening

A business must be willing to produce strong relationships with others in the same environment. Listening is often the first step toward understanding and respecting the concerns that people have. There are several ways to listen to others:

1. Regular meetings are recommended.

An HR member should meet with employees regularly. The needs and demands of the employees should be noted. You can have regular meetings on a quarterly or monthly basis if needed. Be aware of how those people respond and that they are comfortable and respond readily.

2. Be prepared for any conversations with your employees.

Many HR professionals will be easier to trust when they are prepared for what their employees have to say. An HR expert must understand that an employee might have very specific concerns or needs. Employees will also feel more confident when they notice that their HR leaders are paying attention to them. This shows respect.

3. The HR expert needs to ask questions.

The technologies and other concepts being supported should be analyzed based on what might work best in an environment. Look at the things you have learned in the discussion. What do you feel would work the best when making positive changes for you and the employee in the future? There needs to be a way for both sides to agree and be on the same page.

4. Recognize that it often takes time to reach an agreement.

A long-term relationship requires patience. The people in the relationship have to talk with each other and share their thoughts or concerns. People who are willing to share their thoughts and ideas with one another are more likely to succeed.

5. Analyze company goals.

The goals include short and long-term efforts. The HR expert has to know what can be done for each person in the work environment to succeed and thrive. Compliments should be offered when appropriate.

Additional Considerations to Manage Relationships

1. A Human Resources professional has to be approachable.

An HR expert who wants to be respected must be easy to approach. Courtesy has to be expressed in the work environment. A person who is not courteous and respectful might be difficult for people to respect or approach.

2. Customer service has to be offered.

Customer service is always critical to a business. The control must be followed between the HR professional and the employees and customers alike. Part of this includes recognizing the needs of employees and customers.

3. The HR professional has to be an advocate for the employees.

An employee needs an advocate in order to know they are supported. The job of an advocate is to listen and to provide feedback based on what is happening. The feedback will entail understanding what should be done when responding to the needs that a person holds. You can work as an advocate for anyone provided that you understand what someone wants to do and how well those ideas one has may be followed.

In many cases, an advocate helps to amplify the voice of a person who has a concern. In this case, an HR professional can forward concerns surrounding conditions in the workplace or processes involved and find ways to resolve the issues.

4. A team should be easy to build.

Team building is vital for ensuring that relationships are effective. The correct behaviors for a group should also be explored based on what might be right for the entity. The internal culture within the workplace will be easier to facilitate when the team that needs to be built is supported by management.

5. Contacts have to be made.

HR professionals must establish smart networks where people can help others based on certain concerns that may develop. Knowing where to go for help or advice in the workplace is vital. The effort should be about recognizing what everyone involved requires and how well the plans involved may be supported.

Plans for Senior Professionals

Senior HR professionals must work with the following concepts about how relationships may be established and how they may be maintained and supported in the long-term:

1. Unique metrics have to be established.

Metrics can entail anything from employee turnover ratios to reviews of expenses surrounding how people might find employees. This includes looking at the cost of acquiring talent or the amount of time needed to get that talent established. The metrics should be relevant to understanding how well an environment is to be supported.

2. Networking is vital for success.

The network is a concept involving how people are to establish relationships with others outside a group. An HR expert may link to other professionals in one business or organization and establish strong connections where many people can help one another. The extended team approach makes it easier for a company to progress with the company's plans.

3. Communication with stakeholders is needed.

Negotiations with stakeholders can make a difference in the work process. Such negotiations may involve reviewing what people want and how well ideas are to be followed. You can use communications to negotiate ideas and to decide on the best strategies that a business can use.

4. A focus on customer service is necessary.

Relationships should be planned based on customer service. The things that the business will do will be noticed by the customers. Therefore, there is a need to work with strong customer service standards. To do this, there needs to be a sense of purpose and support. This includes a review of the general values of the company that personnel must follow. A strong commitment to these values is critical to success.

Sometimes the customer service will have an extensive hiring or training campaign. You might have to hire more people and offer extensive support. The messages you convey have to be consistent.

5. There has to be a way to resolve conflicts in the workplace.

Every workplace is going to have some conflict. This is an unavoidable truth. The HR department must recognize how conflict can be controlled and/or resolved. A senior HR professional must also receive proper training to resolve conflicts.

6. Relationships that are new have to be developed.

The development of a strong relationship is critical to success in management. Talking people through their development and sharing helpful suggestions are critical for a business to thrive. You can also enhance your relationships by understanding what people require to do their work properly and efficiently.

Consultation

Consultation involves providing advice to others in the workplace. You can use the consultation to review the things that people are doing and to advise them on what might be corrected.

You have to evaluate the challenges that are in your business. You must notice where your business is going based on what you've planned. You should also devise simple solutions for the workplace based on what is appropriate and easy for the workforce to implement.

You also need to use consultation with customers to determine if they are satisfied and if they are not, what suggestions do they have to improve interaction with the company.

Problem-Solving

The consultation should entail discussing problems in the workplace and how these issues can be resolved. You can talk with the workforce about the concerns they have and what needs to be done to resolve these issues. There are a few steps to use to resolve problems:

1. Identify the problem.

Review the problem and determine possible solutions for the issue. You can work with a committee to elicit suggestions that might be effective solutions.

2. Itemize the solutions that might work.

These solutions can be for immediate remedy or taking into account what could happen in the future. You should be predictive in what you plan, but be realistic about what may happen in the future.

3. Determine the criteria that are appropriate for the solutions.

Make sure you have a smart plan in mind that will benefit the company. Every solution you plan should be compared with the criteria established for the company.

4. After you evaluate the solutions based on the criteria, choose a solution to implement.

Communicate with your employees so they will feel comfortable with the solution to the problem.

5. Decide how to implement the changes.

The solutions are going to impact your entire company and the employees. You could plan a pilot program to analyze the quality of your solution. You can expand the pilot to cover the entire workforce if you find the effort involved has worked and you are satisfied with the result.

6. Measure the results.

The results of the implemented solution should be checked and measured. See if the results are meeting the expectations you had. Anything that suggests the plans are not working well might indicate the need for additional changes.

Coaching the Workforce

You can develop healthy relationships with others during coaching sessions. Here are a few tips to use when coaching others:

1. Plan the coaching sessions in advance. Decide who is going to be the recipients of the coaching lessons you have planned.

2. Listen to the people you're planning to coach. You should take notes on what they are saying.

3. Determine which roles will change and how they will change.

4. Be willing to work with other coaches. Teamwork is always the best option.

5. Consider the effort of everyone involved. Consultation should involve saving those people time and effort.

6. Identify the technology that may be beneficial and improve efficiency.

7. Use a team approach when implementing changes. A team approach shows that you recognize the concerns of others.

8. Ask open-ended questions to gage the understanding of the people receiving coaching.

9. Follow up with the workforce regarding the coaching they received to determine if the coaching was adequate and useful.

Senior Professional Plans

1. Managing Talent

You can utilize services from various talent-based organizations to find the best people to hire for the task at hand.

2. Be willing to listen.

Listen to your workers to understand what they feel might be appropriate for the work efforts in question. People will feel as though you are on the same page when they recognize that their contribution is worthwhile and their opinions count.

3. Have a vision for the future.

You should review your capital and then plan your efforts based on what you feel is appropriate. Your human capital should be reviewed based on their skills and educational potentials. Use your present workforce to allow for promotions.

Enhancing Your Return on Investment

Every senior HR professional has to use the consultation to enhance the overall return on investment.

1. Psychological impacts can influence what a person does. A consultation should be planned based on how they review and resolve problems.

2. Many environmental factors may influence the work produced, such as air quality, heat, air-conditioning, sound, lighting, etc.

3. Physiological elements include the time of day, how the work breaks affect workers, how they feel about supervision and if it is fair or too harsh. Decide what things could be changed to accommodate the workers and make work more productive and efficient.

4. Emotions are important to consider. You have to review how people in your workplace are managing different activities and functions. The key is

to review how well the people in the workplace are motivated and whether they are willing to conform to the workload or not.

5. Sociological changes can make an impact in the workplace. Some of these changes may include how some workers might work with others and how they are going to manage different forms of authority.

Working with Analytical Tools

A part of your work in managing your investment is to see how well the analytical tools you are using work. All HR professionals, particularly those who are in senior management, must understand and recognize the resources they can use. There are many programs available that help businesses to identify many considerations surrounding how the business functions. Arcadia Data, RapidMiner, SciPy, Weka Data Mining, and Orange Data Mining are among the top programs people can use to find analytical data surrounding many functions.

An HR professional may also need to work with an SQL database. The Structured Query Language is necessary for arranging databases and making them as easy to follow as possible. You can use an SQL database for keeping your content arranged accordingly. The key about using an SQL database is that the days where you'd have to use a basic spreadsheet program for managing your analytics needs are over. You need to work with advanced programs to make it easier for you to analyze data and to find the best possible connections.

The Most Prominent Liabilities

Every HR professional must recognize the liabilities of managing different evaluation functions. SHRM states that these particular concerns can be significant threats if not handled properly:

1. FLSA violations. The Fair Labor Standards Act states that people are entitled to certain rights in the workplace. This includes rules surrounding overtime pay, limits on how much work someone would regularly complete, and various considerations surrounding child labor. Any claims that a company is not following FLSA standards can suggest that you are not treating your employees fairly.

2. <u>Class action lawsuits</u>. Such lawsuits may be initiated for any reason relating to improper activities or illegal actions in the workplace. Such acts may be threatening to the quality and viability of the business.

3. <u>FMLA violations</u>. The Family and Medical Leave Act provides people with the opportunity to take time off of work without consequence. These include family medical emergencies, the birth of a child, or any other significant issues surrounding one's family life and health.

4. <u>Whistleblowers</u>. A whistleblower is a person within the business who sounds an alarm about something illegal happening in the workplace. In most cases, the whistleblower is anonymous and can cite evidence surrounding the illegal activity. Sometimes the actions are improper ones that a business is not aware are illegal.

5. <u>Data breaches</u>. Data in the workplace may be exposed by someone. This could be information about private business activities or about the employees themselves. In the worst cases, this might be credit card information or other details surrounding customers. HR professionals should be able to review how these situations are to be resolved if they occur. This is to provide the public with a sense of trust over what is being done to protect their information.

6. <u>Social media activities</u>. This could be some bad reviews that people post or stories about how a business operates. An HR professional must notice how people can be contacted and how social media-related issues may develop. The use of proper social media experts in the workplace may assist in how any situation can be handled.

7. <u>Sexual harassment</u>. In addition to creating a hostile and uncomfortable environment, sexual harassment causes a company or someone in the company to experience legal action. This is due to such actions being a violation of civil rights laws.

8. <u>Alternative work activities</u>. People often participate in things like telecommuting or job-sharing. Outsourcing can be a concern when people interact with one another or fail to interact appropriately.

Critical Evaluation

A critical evaluation requires effort in analyzing the data and how you're going to use it. You have to understand the data that you are gathering, how you're going to gather that data, and how you will analyze the data. Then you need to make decisions according to what the data reveals.

1. Make the right decisions.

You need to decide what would work for your business. The goal is to review the information as thoroughly and carefully as possible. This is vital for your success and how your business works.

2. Consider the laws.

Many workplace laws are going to influence your evaluation. Such laws may impact how your payroll is managed or how people are hired and treated. You have to review these laws based on what is appropriate for your work environment. You must also predict how your business is going to adapt to the changes in laws.

3. Be able to move the knowledge you have in one field to another.

You would have to decide how you're going to transfer knowledge between tasks. Being able to convey information to other parties is essential. You need to let the people in the workplace know about any changes or other concerns that are developing.

Reviewing and Collecting Data

There are a few things to do surrounding data:

1. Determine the process to use to gather critical data.

You have to identify the information you require and how it can be gathered.

2. Analyze the data after you gather it.

You must analyze the data and then test it for accuracy and relevance.

3. Identify the best practices for work based on the data collected.

Determine the practices you want to follow based on how your business operates. Review the best practices that you wish to follow.

Any data from other companies open to the public can also be used to help you make your decisions. You can always review what's appropriate, but an alternative or two might help too. Your work should be planned based on what is sensible for your business.

4. Analyze specific indicators that make an impact.

Notice the leading indicators about how productive your business is or how people are engaging in certain activities and functions. The recruiting, retention and budget considerations may also be explored at this time.

Large Amounts of Data

There's a chance that you will have a massive amount of data gathered. You have to sort and prioritize the data based on what is appropriate versus how secure and sensible the content is.

After you gather and sort the data, you need to decide where your business is going, what points are the most effective, and what opportunities are available. You must also look at any flaws in the operation of your business that you've discovered based on your research. You will identify the problem, define the concerns, and then find the data needed for resolving the issue. You can then plan your work with a solution based on the data you have gathered.

Senior HR Professionals

1. Maintain your knowledge.

A senior HR professional has to be fully aware of what is happening in the organization and how positive changes can be made.

2. Make recommendations based on your analysis.

Recommendations are needed to identify how effective certain plans might be. You have to look at the impact that your data will have on your organization.

3. Look for information.

The search for information should be a full review of whatever might be necessary for your business.

4. Support the improvement initiatives that you want to implement.

The improvement initiatives require effort to understanding the goals of the company versus what resources you have and how you're going to make changes. You should also support changes surrounding your data involved with the content you want to follow.

Your work as a senior HR professional should include designing new improvement initiatives. Hiring someone to assist you with the implementation of changes can be to manage the business.

5. Communicate the data analysis with others.

An HR professional must explain the data to others in order to implement the necessary changes for the benefit of the company as a whole in order to have the best possible results.

6. Create policies surrounding the evaluated data.

Look at your policies based on the data and decide how relevant they are to the workplace. Creating policies will help in planning work projects so they are effectively completed.

You have to notice what your business is doing versus how the business is changing attitudes and actions. Any technological, political, social, legal, or environmental changes in the workplace should be reviewed. You might have to make changes to your plans based on those factors.

You must also look at the competition and other influencing factors that might impact your business. You can review the competition based on factors like what people prefer when finding products or services and what they can purchase to make the most of their budgets.

7. Challenge assumptions.

Your assumptions might be unfair or unrealistic. You need to look at assumptions based on the surroundings around you. For instance, one business might be triggered by economic factors or from changes in the services customers might want. Plan to challenge the assumptions you develop while finding ways to keep these from being a threat to the development of the company.

Global and Cultural Effectiveness

There is a need for people in all workplaces to be aware of different cultures and how they function. Global and cultural effectiveness focuses on understanding how you can work in a global environment and how you're able to manage a diverse workforce. You should also advocate for a more diverse setting.

1. Adapt to many situations in the workplace.

You are expected to work with various situations that might be a challenge for management. You need to adapt to other cultures and respect the people of those cultures if they are part of your workforce.

The cultural differences cause different cultural situations. For instance:

- Different parts of the world have unique laws regarding work standards regarding how much time off an employee is allowed.

- There are rules on the hours that people can work per day.

- There are rules for how people conduct meetings or other activities in the workplace.

2. You must also be open to suggestions from the workforce.

It is often difficult to adapt to certain cultures. You should avoid judging people based on your standards. Listening to others and understanding their needs can be vital for the business.

Show a sincere appreciation for everyone you are working with. You are a person who recognizes the concerns or issues that people have.

3. You have to show a sense of trust in everyone.

Working with people who are different from you might be difficult for you to manage. You have to believe that everyone you are working with is helpful and is available to give you the assistance you need. Trust entails noting the things that people can do for you in the workplace. Developing a sense of trust ensures that everyone understands what needs to be done and when.

4. Encourage inclusion.

The concept of promoting inclusion is ensuring that all people are welcome in your environment. You will need to promote a sense of acceptance for all groups involved in your business.

Senior Professionals

1. Review the competencies of individuals from different cultures.

It will be necessary to consider your strategy for the work that involves employees of various cultures. Is there a need to make changes to accommodate the skills needed and the workforce you have?

2. Be aware of the economic outlook.

The economic outlook of the world can play a major role in what will happen in your business. You need to notice how plans may need to change because of outside factors that might influence your business. The attitudes and actions of people in different cultures may be based on the economic pressures that they are facing.

3. Review trends based on cultures.

Whether it entails social or political change, many cultures will evolve. Sometimes groups may be open to new ideas. In other cases, people of a culture may become defensive. Such impacts may directly influence what you wish to do. Noting how a culture will evolve and change is vital to recognize what changes will have to be made to accommodate those cultures.

4. Identify a vision that promotes success between cultures.

You need to have a vision of what will work when interacting with a different cultural entity.

Some points to note include:

- Is a hierarchy needed for leadership or is an egalitarian process necessary?

- Deciding on a consensual or top-down plan for managing work

- Seeing that trust is established based on the relationships that are developed

- Seeing how specific standards may apply to persuade people or if a holistic approach is best

- Understanding how disagreement can be resolved

Establishing a Relationship

You will need to notice what you are doing when getting your relationship ready and easy to operate. These are aspects of keeping a relationship running that have to be explored well:

1. Be willing to understand the concerns that people have. This includes never making any assumptions about what people might be thinking or feeling.

2. Always keep an open mind when looking at what someone might be doing or thinking. This includes keeping stereotypes from being a burden.

3. Think about attending a networking event where you can interact with people from other cultures. You can use such an event to experience many things surrounding what's around where you are.

4. Always keep your word in the relationships you're trying to plan out. Show that there is a sense of interest or comfort in what you wish to do with your work.

5. Never assume that the people involved in a situation have negative intent. There is always going to be a sense of positivity among the people who are going to work with you.

Communication

It is critical for you to be able to communicate with others in the HR field. Communication is being able to convey messages and ideas to others effectively. You must exchange information professionally and accurately. Being capable of listening to others and your ability to pay attention to people and respect their needs is also vital for success.

1. Clarity is a necessity for communication.

Whatever you say must be clear and simple to follow. A communicator must convey a message geared to a specific receiver while encouraging feedback. The content of the message has to be accurate and consistent. Confidentiality must also be established to promote trust.

2. The people involved have to listen to each other.

The best communicator is someone who is capable of listening. An HR expert has to review the things that are being said and confirm them. Some nonverbal language like appearing receptive and not being bored and disinterested in the conversation is important to note.

3. The information should be prioritized.

Decide what information is the most important to convey and keep the conversation from diverging. An agenda keeps everyone on track.

4. Encourage constructive feedback.

Feedback is useful, but it has to be constructive. This part of HR work includes communicating with your employees what they are doing right versus what might be producing errors.

5. The message should be positive.

Be direct and honest, while also being open to considering ideas from others. You can be effective by listening to people.

6. Recognize your audience.

You have to use your emotional intelligence (EI) to find out what people might want. The EI refers to how well you recognize your audience. Recognize the demands that people have and how much help they might require so you will know what is suitable and sensible.

7. Lead the meetings.

You will have to plan the agenda for a meeting based on the clear goals that you wish to establish. A timeframe for the meeting can be set that is appropriate. You should allow some time for answering questions. Any decisions or ideas should be discussed at the end. You can always send a summary to the people who attended later.

Senior Professionals

1. Be willing to talk with stakeholders.

While it is important for HR experts to talk with their co-workers, senior HR teams have to also to talk with the stakeholders who have a vested interest in the company and its viability.

The open-ended nature of the communication should be planned to be effective.

2. Receiving feedback.

A senior professional needs to solicit feedback. Getting feedback from others helps you to identify what people are doing and what they might think about certain plans. You can use this feedback to change your plans or modify them.

Think about the responses and if it is identical to what you were expecting. Identify any confusion involved in the message you gave and what the audience heard.

3. Framing the Discussion

Framing is setting a reason for communication. The message should be clear. Framing is explaining the objective of communication. You must also discuss the benefits of communication.

Correct Methods of Communication

There are eight formats that HR specialists can use:

1. Face-to-Face

A face-to-face is most appropriate when talking with one or two people at a time. A face-to-face provides immediate feedback and makes it easier for nonverbal communication to be noticed. You can use this personalized communication if you're going to find ways to resolve conflicts or other issues, including issues that might be very sensitive in nature.

2. Phone Call

A phone call gives people an easy opportunity to ask questions. This also works well for when you need to talk about confidential things. Some misunderstanding could arise because there are no visual cues.

3. Voicemail

Voicemail is useful when people are difficult to contact. This method of communication is not recommended because of the negatives involved, not to mention the 'phone tag' that could occur.

4. Email

An email gives the sender the ability to send attachments and media files with your email message. You also have the option to send an email to many parties. You must be careful of the wording of your email and the feeling that is produced.

5. Brief Messages

Today's technology has made it easier for people to get in touch through brief messages. You can use Google Hangouts to Skype to any other chat program you want. Texting by phone helps but only use this when you really need to convey messages as soon as possible.

Brief message services are best to announce specific information to the public. This includes anything promotional in nature. Emergency data can also be sent out through a brief message; this may include alerts surrounding significant concerns in the workplace that have to be resolved immediately.

6. Social Media

Social media is helpful because it has a massive reach. You can get a social media message sent out to anyone who follows you online. The variety of social media avenues you have to work with providing you with many opportunities for reaching people. You can use social media to target specific audiences or a casual audience on Instagram or a formal professional group on LinkedIn among other places.

You could post things like surveys and promotional messages. You can also produce private social media messages between you and certain people who are on specific media sites.

7. Written Documents

A written document can include anything from a handbook or pamphlet to a larger PDF you might attach to an email. The written document takes time to prepare but can provide full documentation that needs to be shared with a larger audience.

8. Oral Discussions

You can have oral discuss with groups of any size. You can include visuals or handouts and even include video files. The oral presentation lets you receive immediate feedback and can help you to adjust your message as necessary.

Chapter 3 – People

This segment of the study guide focuses on people - how you're going to hire people and how you are going to engage with your employees.

Talent Acquisition and Retention

The talent acquisition requires knowing how to find the right people that can help a business. Retention is finding out what is required to keep the people you've hired.

Staffing and Finding the Right Talent

You'll have to work hard with others to see what talent is available. Staffing challenges can be frustrating and there are several issues that will directly impact the acquisition of new talent.

First, you have to look at the people who are available based on changes. Demographics and trends in your field of business can change. You might experience a lack of skilled labor.

You might experience certain economic or business cycles that will influence the availability of skilled labor. Sometimes it might be difficult to find people due to a shortage of educational opportunities for young people – grants not available, funding for teachers curtailed, etc.

The employees already on staff may not have the skills necessary to apply for the new positions or they may not feel motivated to apply. You might consider hiring from outside the country if talented people are not available at home. This will require research into the visa requirements for the new hires.

Technology may have changed and certain functions in the workplace now require new skilled workers or re-educating the existing staff. This requires a new look at finances that are available.

Branding

Some people might be very positive about your business based on the things you have done in the past. You can use social media to brand your business, or you can use other advertising campaigns. These may help to make your business more inviting and interesting to the public.

You can also create an EVP or Employee Value Proposition as a part of your brand. EVP is a series of benefits that people can get based on their work. This includes the skills and functions that one has and the length of an employee's employment with the company

When branding your business for employment purposes, you have to show people what you are offering and that what you have to provide is useful. You might need to make changes for making your business visible. You may also develop an action plan based on the changes that you want to utilize. A thorough evaluation of your business practices will help you to create new plans.

Documenting Your Job

An HR professional has to market a job to the public for people to take the opening seriously. You can create a job description that illustrates the things that you wish to highlight at a time. The documentation has to follow a template.

Your job description may include the following details:

1. The job details including part-time, full-time, or casual, temporary or on-call

2. Pay scale – hourly or monthly

3. Educational requirements

4. Skills required

5. Signing bonus, if applicable

6. Physical factors involved with a job

7. Environmental factors of the job when working in the field

8. Work week hours and details of breaks and overtime pay rates.

9. Benefits and compensation packages according to employment status

10. Probationary period, if applicable

Methods of Recruiting

There are two basic types of recruiting: internal and external hiring.

Internal recruiting is the most common form of recruiting and is finding new workers from within the business. Giving your present employees the opportunity to take the next step forward in their careers is an excellent way of boosting morale and rewarding those who have been exemplary employees.

External recruiting is going outside the business to find new people. You might be able to attract employees who are presently working elsewhere or who are just now entering the workforce. You can use job boards, social media, or your company's website to encourage people to apply. Referrals from clients, vendors, and customers among other outside parties should also be considered.

Analyzing How You Are Hiring

Analyze how you are hiring based on how quickly positions are being filled and how many interviews were required to find the appropriate candidate.

Check on factors like demographics, individual groups being hired, the cost of each hire, and many other factors. You can also review the number of days that you are spending filling positions. An analysis of this measure will help you identify how you are hiring people and if you need to make any changes to the hiring process.

Selecting the Talent

The selection process should include a review of the talent you need for the positions you have open. A screening process has to be devised.

1. Knowledge and Skill

You can review the knowledge that people hold based on prior work experience, how educated they are, their technical skills, how well they can communicate with others, and any specialized training they have had.

2. Behaviors

All people engage in various behaviors. Some people may be motivated to keep working hard and will have the drive to succeed. Reliability is also important to consider.

3. Compatibility

Compatibility refers to how well a person is able to adhere to certain standards in the workplace. A person has to be compatible with others they are working with and be receptive to suggestions from superiors.

Warning Signs

Be aware of some warning signs presented by some applicants. Those who do not have recent experience and have no reliable references available could be a concern. Anyone who has had a number of jobs in a short period of time could also be a point for concern.

The Interview Process

You can conduct a structured interview that entails basic questions. You can also conduct an unstructured interview that focuses on a more freewheeling general discussion to discover details informally. A behavioral interview may also focus on the ways someone might respond to particular situations.

A group interview may be conducted if you plan on hiring people who are going to work in large team situations. The interview helps gage how well people may act when tasked to complete certain jobs. You could also hold a stress interview that focuses on how well a person might handle high-pressure situations.

Employee Engagement

Employees need to feel they are being supported and understood. You can use this to where you can review what your employees need and how they are going to be supported in the work environment. The plan helps determine what the people in the workforce might benefit from the most.

You can use three types of engagement efforts in your work. A trait-based approach focuses on the particular personality points that you want to review. A stage approach involves looking at the influence of the workplace and how it might influence what happens at work. A behavioral engagement plan entails looking at the possible levels of satisfaction that a person might have after completing certain tasks.

A company that engages with the employees can be more productive and profitable. Employees will feel as though they are welcome in their environments and will be less likely to be absent from work.

What Drives Engagement?

Engagement is driven by four factors:

1. The work one does and the development that comes with the work

2. The stability of the workplace and the situation at hand

3. Rewards that may be available

4. The flow of communication

Forms of Leadership

Engagement starts with effective leadership where the people in the workplace feel as though they are being supported. The types of leadership can be:

1. Transformational

A transformational leader is a person who identifies the changes that are needed in the workplace and how they are to be made. The leader inspires the workers and executes changes with the engagement of the workers.

2. Authentic

An authentic leader will produce strong relationships with the workers and focuses on ethical standards for work.

3. Supportive

A supportive leader identifies the path and supports the workers as changes are made.

Challenges

There are many problems that might keep engagement from working. Global competition may create difficult goals requiring a revamping of present goals for the business. Some new technology may have to be implemented for a business to go forward. The economic conditions in an area can trigger difficulties in recruiting new employees.

Reviewing Engagement

1. Gather information on how people are engaging with you.

Consider the people who are actively engaging with management. These include people who are willingly doing what they can to support the business. You can conduct employee surveys to see how the workers feel about their working environments and other aspects of employment. Focus groups may also be held to discover employees' level of satisfaction. Individual interviews can also be conducted with various people in the workplace.

2. Analyze the results of the interviews.

You can review the results of your communications with your workers to reveal what they might be thinking about the work environment and if they have concerns or issues surrounding what they are doing in the workplace. As you look at these results, you can determine the actions you wish to take. These actions may be based on what you feel is appropriate to help your employees and give them the opportunities they are looking for.

3. Engage with your employees when changes are being made.

Talk with your employees as you move toward making changes. Ask them about their thoughts surrounding the changes you are going to implement. Being able to engage with the employees during the process makes it easier for the changes to be made and allows the employees involved to feel as though they are being valued and recognized.

Motivation Theories

There are certain needs that motivate a person or group of people to want to attain a certain goal.

The different behaviors and actions of each person in the workplace are signs that there will be certain things that influence what a person will do or will be willing to do.

There are many other motivation theories:

1. Maslow's Hierarchy of Needs

Maslow uses a pyramid to express the needs that people have. People need physiological concerns like food, water, and warmth at the beginning. After that, a person needs safety and security. Psychological needs like relationships with others and a sense of esteem or accomplishment come next. After that, people will be able to attain self-fulfillment by engaging in certain actions.

2. Motivation-Hygiene Theory

Herzberg states that people have two types of needs. First, there are extrinsic factors that focus on job security, working condition, supervision, and managing one's relationships with others. Second, there are intrinsic motivations, such as recognition and personal growth.

3. Behavioral Reinforcement Theory

Skinner cites that behavioral reinforcement theory is recognizing how behaviors among people in the workplace can be shaped. The behaviors can be shaped by receiving certain rewards or punishments based on whether they do things right or wrong. The actions following those behaviors can direct people to want to continue those behaviors or to avoid those actions altogether.

Managing Performances by Appraisals

Performance management is vital to identify how workers are effectively engaging in the right activities. The management reviews the work based on the performance standards that have been established. Appraisals may be held to identify what and who needs improvement and what issues have been identified.

A review of the work can be reviewed through the behaviorally anchored rating system (BARS) to identify certain actions being taken and certain work demands and how the work is being accomplished.

A self-assessment is given to each employee so they can assess their own capabilities and achievements. You need to ensure the instructions for a self-assessment are followed and that people are encouraged to be honest in answering questions.

Different errors may develop in the performance appraisal process. These errors include the following issues:

- Halo – a person does well in one area and therefore gets high ratings elsewhere

- Horn – a person is weak in one area and has low ratings elsewhere

- Recency – excess emphasis is placed on a certain event

- Primacy – earlier performances are weighted heavier

- Leniency – a person is too relaxed in grading people

- Bias – a review's bias impacts the perspective

- Contrast – the review is based on comparisons with others in the same workplace

Retention

Retention is the ability to keep employees who are already hired and working in the workplace.

Your business will reach the break-even point for new-hire retention at some point. This is calculated by taking the monthly value of a new hire and dividing it by the cost of recruiting and hiring for that position. A shorter period means that you can afford to allow for employee turnover. However, it is better to retain your employees in general regardless of the break-even point.

Retention can be attained by providing sensible approaches to engage with your employees. You can provide regular training services to increase the employees' skill level. Reward and recognition systems, communication with your workers, and a general work-life balance are always an incentive.

Learning and Development

Your employees must be given opportunities to learn and develop their skills. People will feel accepted and willing to work if they are given opportunities to learn new and unique skills.

Trainability is a concept that entails managing the employee's motivation to accept training and to learn new things. A person must be ready to learn and to go forward with the work that is being introduced.

Three Types of Learners

Three types of adult learners :

1. Auditory

An auditory learner is one who learns more and learns easily by listening to people speaking to them. These people can identify instructions and details when people directly talk to them. Lectures and other forms of verbal instructions are easily learned by the auditory learner.

2. Visual

A visual learner does better when visually observing actions or by reading. This type of learner can learn detailed functions of machines by either hands-on or by watching someone's actions. To-do lists and flip charts can work for visual learners.

3. Kinesthetic

A kinesthetic worker is someone who focuses on a hands-on approach together with some auditory and visual aspects. The main goal is to learn a routine.

Obstacles to Learning

Many obstacles can get in the way and hinder learning. Situational issues or institutional concerns occur when people see procedures or activities that exclude them or make them feel as though certain activities or ideas are not appropriate for them. Dispositional obstacles may involve attitudes that a person has about the self-based on prior experiences.

Learning Styles

Every person in the workplace has a distinct learning style. This includes cases where a person might need extra time to learn things. A person may experience increasing returns when one learns gradually over time. Decreasing returns is when a person is a fast learner at the start and the rate of learning eventually declines. Some people may also experience a plateau where one has learned all they can until they have an "a-ha moment" where everything comes together and that person learns more in a short period.

Designing Learning Practices

The ADDIE model will help you produce a sensible training program.

1. Analysis

The analysis stage is reviewing the group that will receive training. The review can involve an analysis of how well people might be receptive to new ideas and how they can take advantage of them. Sometimes a cultural influence might make it harder for particular people to learn certain ideas easily.

2. Design

The design process is identifying what things need to be presented. Identify goals for the trainees and objectives to meet along the way. You can review the styles of learning people may be comfortable with. A look at cultures among the people in the workplace may also help.

3. Development

The development stage is a review of the specific training methods that may be used. You can plan unique activities for how people are to learn. You may consider instructor-led training or on-the-job training. Learning portals that people can access online may also be used. The use of social media may also be useful for trainees to learn and be in tune with whatever it is they are studying.

4. Implementation

The fourth part is putting the plan in effect. You can use a pilot test to test the program on a few trainees to see how well the plan is working and then revise your content for a larger group. You also have to find the right instructors to implement your training plan. Instructions to the trainees before the training begins are also required.

5. Evaluation

The ADDIE process ends with a review of how well the trainees learned the material. How did the targets react? What did they learn? Has their behavior changed? What specific results are you anticipating from the trainees?

Developing People

Several steps may be used on the HR level for helping people to evolve:

1. Identify proper mentoring programs that may be used in the workplace. These include programs that help people learn more about leadership in work environments.

2. Establish a review of the training needs people have. This includes seeing what people will want to learn as they progress in their studies.

3. Perform an appropriate assessment identify many opportunities surrounding the work of the trainees.

4. Complete regular training sessions.

Rewards

Unique rewards can be offered to your workers for the jobs that they do and how well they complete them. Rewards can include compensation for your workers as well as special benefits recognition for their work, and the ability to help them develop further.

Compensation refers to the payments that people receive including bonuses for certain things. Benefits are non-monetary payments like insurance, vacation, income protection, retirement benefits, and profit sharing. Perks are often useful but are also discretionary. These perks may include things given to people who do well or have seniority. Such perks include company cars, allowances for travel and meals, and the choice of hours for when one wishes to work.

You can plan a rewards program for your workers to encourage them to continue to contribute to your workplace. A program should motivate people and provide them with security for the work that they do. You must also ensure that the rewards you offer are cost-effective and that your business can realistically offer them. More importantly, you have to ensure these benefits are legal.

Reward Strategies

You can use many strategies for producing rewards that your employees will appreciate:

1. Review rewards based on your standards and according to the law.

The rewards you offer need to be relevant to the needs of your employees and be ones that people might appreciate or support. The rewards should also be planned to where they work with local laws or standards.

2. Identify cultural points.

Some rewards or benefits may be more valuable to certain people depending on the situation. You have to notice how these cultural aspects are going to influence what people want from their rewards. Such rewards have to be simple and useful while still being interesting to the people who are receiving them.

3. Review your competition.

Some people might try to hire people away from unique rewards that are more beneficial. Take a look at what they offer and see if you can match those rewards. This will ensure they don't defect and go elsewhere.

4. Be aware of economic factors.

Economic factors include recessions and other global turndowns that might make it harder for you to afford some of the things you want to provide. You'll have to review your rewards based on affordability.

5. Know the taxation standards where you live.

You can identify the terms surrounding the benefits and determine what tax rules are to be imposed on them.

Designing Compensation

You can review a position based on the quality of the job. An analysis of a job can be completed based on the qualifications that the incumbents have. You can also compare other positions based on where your business is.

Compensation Systems

You can have a single system for base pay for task-based jobs where people are paid based on rank or seniority. You can also use a time-based system where a person's pay rate is increased based on the schedule of work. A performance-based system is based on how well people are performing with the best-performing employees being more likely to be paid more.

Compensation may also increase based on the cost of living in an area. You must also notice the compensation that you are contemplating based on any adverse conditions of the job. A time-based differential pay can be implemented based on the number of hours worked in addition to regular hours. Geographic differentials, like isolation pay, may be used to reward people who work in places that are hard to access.

Health Benefits

Health benefits are among the most common that companies provide their workers. Private health insurance may be provided alongside assistance programs. A wellness program may also be used to encourage people to stay healthy by offering gym memberships, programs to manage health issues, and other considerations for managing different health-related issues.

Severance Packages

Severance packages may also be included for cases when a worker is fired or made redundant. Occasions, when a business is shrinking due to an economic turndown or from a part of the organization no longer being necessary, can cause the need to decrease the number of employees. You might have to plan a severance package that includes pay based on the length of service or payments for unused benefits. The assistance should also be provided to people to help them find new jobs. Remember that these can only be provided to people if they were removed from their positions through no fault of their own.

Chapter 4 – Organization

The organization of a business is critical for its operation. You must ensure that the HR department at your workplace is organized to where everyone can make the most out of the work they are planning. There exists a need to look at how well a business operates and how it may function based on where it goes. You will explore in this chapter how HR functions are to be organized and how your workforce can be supported as necessary among other factors.

Structure of HR

The human resources function in the workplace is designed to support many activities and all employees. You are required to advise people, provide records, and control the information being given to the employees and the government. Considerations for people being replaced by machines in the Industrial Revolution, outsourcing in the age of global competition, and legal compliance following the Civil Rights era have all contributed to changes in human resources.

Today's HR departments can be divided into segments that cater to particular functions. There are administrative services relating to how records are managed and gathered, operational services surrounding the recruiting and employee relations, strategic operations and how a business is different from the competition.

Today, an organization has to be highly accountable for what it does. Part of this includes ensuring a business can adapt to changes in society and make changes and compensation for those changes within the company.

General Business Functions

The HR department has to follow many standards for action:

1. Finances and Budgeting

The finances of a business are based on sales, interest, production, payroll, and other factors.

A zero-based budget is a budget that justifies all expenses. An incremental budget can be changed based on what was spent earlier. A formula can be used for deciding how to plan a sensible budget and reconcile it with production.

2. Marketing and Sales

Marketing requires promoting your business to others. Sales come from the people who enjoy the products or services that were marketed to them. You would have to go through this aspect of the business to ensure you have the funds needed for allowing the HR department to stay active and operational.

3. Operations

Operations refer to how services or goods are produced, thus allowing sales to happen. This includes keeping track of inventory, controlling sales, and maintaining excellent customer service.

4. Information Technology

IT is designed to allow data to be shared between many departments or groups in the same organization. You can use IT to keep track of everything that happens within the company so that everyone in management is aware of all transactions.

5. Research and Development

Research and development is an aspect of running a business that entails reviewing how your business can improve. R&D often relates to making a business more modern. The use of technology can help in this area.

Designing an Organization

There are many critical aspects of a business organization to be well-arranged and functional. There are seven distinct types of organizational efforts that may be used:

1. Departmental – people are divided into separate groups responsible for certain jobs

2. Chain of Command – people report to specific entities in one department

3. Span of Control – many people are going to report to one supervisor

4. Work Specialization – recognizing that people in the workplace have very specific tasks

5. Centralization/Decentralization – one group will be responsible for running the business, or regional or district groups will combine to one large group

6. Matrix – a dual chain of command works with an HR firm reporting to another executive

7. RACI Matrix – one person is responsible for a task, another is accountable for the completion of the task, a third will be consulted, a fourth is informed about the work being performed

These organization plans may be arranged in various ways. A hybrid structure that combines two plans is an alternative.

Organizing the HR Team

An HR leader may be chosen to be the person responsible for designing the HR project. Managers may report to the leader as they are assigned tasks within specific departments or locations. Specialists that focus on very specific functions in the workplace may also report to the managers. Generalists that concentrate on all major areas of operation may also be hired.

You can also plan a shared services approach to handling HR. Shared services entail working with multiple divisions in your work environment. These divisions are responsible for supporting many fields within the company and will keep administrative costs down. It may also be easier for employee data to be tracked.

A center of excellence can also be produced. A center involves a group that focuses on certain skills or technologies. A center of expertise may also be set up to provide people with educational opportunities.

Third-parties may also be hired for handling tasks. Although a third-party is often the last choice, outside groups could be responsible for organizing benefits or planning employment functions.

Measurement Standards

An organization can have its efforts measured by many solutions:

1. Scorecard

An HR scorecard will measure many internal actions and then review the possible outcomes. Measures involving certain actions or ideas associated with them can be employed.

2. Audit

An audit is a review of the HR processes in the workplace. The audit can be conducted regularly. Compliance audits may be held to identify how a business is complying with certain regulations. A best practice review may also look at certain functions compared to what others in the same business are doing. You can also use strategic analysis to see how well certain plans are working. A function-specific audit can determine how well certain tasks are being supported in the workplace.

3. Metrics

You can use metrics based on attendance rates, cost-per-hire, promotional efforts, success ratios, turnover costs and rates, and any vacancy costs. The metrics you use can be specialized based on the industry.

Conducting Negotiations

An HR professional has to be ready to negotiate with parties within or outside of the business. You can use many steps to negotiate:

1. Build strong relationships with others. This includes looking at how you're going to get the trust of others.

2. Exchange information with others.

3. Plan your persuasion points. Decide what to promote or discuss.

4. Make concessions if necessary to reach an agreement.

5. The agreement after the negotiating should be in writing.

Due diligence is needed before negotiations begin. Due diligence entails looking at how you're going to help a business based on the actions that you plan to use.

Strategic Alignment

The strategic alignment involves seeing that the HR department has a defined mission. Part of this might include looking at your organization's history. You can always use objective data to support the alignment of the HR structure.

Steps to Plan an HR Strategy

There are a few useful steps that you can use when planning your HR strategy:

1. Review the big picture.

Your HR strategy must be planned based on the big picture. This includes knowing how effective the work in question is.

2. Plan a SWOT analysis.

The HR strategy can include an analysis based on your strengths, weaknesses, opportunities, and threats. These are all internal and external factors that can have a major impact on the business.

3. Plan an HR analysis based on the current things you are doing.

Your mission statement and vision for your business should be explored in detail. You can also carefully analyze any gaps in what you are doing based on how you are trying to attain and what you want to do in the future.

4. Determine employee issues.

These issues include the current talent needs and available resources in the workforce.

5. Determine goals.

Your goals can be linked to employee issues. You may also use audits or review scorecards to measure how the workforce is working.

6. Plan how to reach the company goals.

Keep the company goals in mind when contemplating any changes. You can always use a Gantt chart to compare how the goals are being met.

Organizational Effectiveness and Development

Organization effectiveness and development or OED involves identifying a problem in the HR field and then finding a solution. The identification then leads to a plan for a type of intervention that will work. You can use this to do anything from developing talent to enhancing the performances of people.

Resolving Problems

OED functions are necessary to review what might be developing and how you are going to fix concerns before they become worse. You can use a few points for resolving these functions based on our OED actions:

1. Behavioral problems

Proper education and strong leadership are needed to resolve conflicts in the workplace. You can also state clear expectations to reduce confusion.

2. Cognitive issues

A cognitive problem occurs when a person does not have enough knowledge to do a job. Training or mentoring is necessary. This can include on-the-job training and coaching.

3. Technological concerns

Technological concerns can develop involving the materials and equipment needed for certain tasks. You might need to educate people about implementing and using new technology.

4. Process-related problems

Processes problem could involve something relating to reporting issues or how well certain assets are being used. Feedback from the workers needs to be reviewed.

5. Cultural concerns

Some cultural concerns may develop. You may look for internal solutions or outside help.

Using OED in HR

There are many aspects surrounding OED for HR professionals to explore:

1. The HR team must develop a strong talent.

2. Plan communication avenues between departments.

3. Offer work planning and job development for employees.

4. Allow for new technology.

You've got plenty of things that you can do when developing OED in your workplace. Here are a few of the solutions you can incorporate:

1. Team Building

An organization is more effective when people work as a team.

2. Decision-Making As a Group

After the team is built, you can establish sensible decisions. A team has many roles, but a group has a defined leader. Everyone in a group is accountable for completing individual tasks. You can have activities like brainstorming. The Delphi requires people producing ideas on their own and then having those ideas refined by the team.

3. Diversity

It has been found that diverse groups tend to be smarter because of their multiple perspectives. People are challenged toward working in unique ways when they are with people who are different.

4. Quality Initiatives

You can also use quality initiatives may include standards that HR groups are to follow. The International Organization for Standardization has established how you can produce quality in the workplace. Such standards include ISO 30400 for HR management terms, ISO 30405 for HR recruitment, and ISO 30409 HR management. You can find information on the specific ISO standards your HR department at www.iso.org.

5. Quality Control Tools

You can use many quality control tools that include cause and effect diagrams, control charts, histograms, Pareto charts, scatter diagrams, and others. The key to quality control is to review any trends you find using these tools.

6. Six Sigma

Six Sigma is working to reduce variation and errors. You'll have to contact a specific Six Sigma expert to get your program up and running.

Workforce Management

Workforce management relates to how you will manage the supply and demand of your company resources.

Restructuring

Restructuring is a process where a workforce is changed in some way. The restructuring process may entail downsizing, a process where a company realizes the demand for its products has diminished. Divestiture may also occur when a business removes portions of its operations and transfers those operations to other parties. A merger may occur to combine one company's operations with another.

Creating a Workforce

The workforce that you will plan should have common values and a strong vision.

You can produce a demand analysis to determine what should be done and any gaps in your workplace may also be identified so you know where your business is and where you want the business to go in the future. Solution analysis is also helpful for when you recognize a problem in the workplace and need to find workable solutions and establish objectives for your workforce.

Staffing

Your staffing plans should have a statement of purpose. The statement includes a review of your job openings and with a plan for hiring. You must also look at your organizational goals and descriptions of the abilities that are necessary for your job vacancies. You can also schedule interviews and discussions with others in the workplace.

Review the candidates based on their qualifications and schedule interviews. You can also use additional screening processes like interviews, written assessments, etc.

Developing Employees and Managing Different Positions

Analyze the talent pool you have within the existing staff and conduct skill assessments.

You can work with various specific strategies after you've determined the skills of your employees. You can plan job-sharing where people will work in one position at different times of the day or week.

Alternative staffing plans could be hiring people who might work beyond the standard 40-hour week. You can hire project employees for specific tasks. These people will be removed from the workforce after a project is finished. You could consider hiring these people after the project is completed if they prove to be an asset.

You can use payrolling to bridge the gap between different full-time employees and project hires.

A temp-to-lease program may also be a solution for bringing in people for a few weeks or months. These are temporary employees and are not entitled to the benefits of full-time employees.

You might also consider relocation for some of these employees to different offices in other markets. Relocation may be needed to help with restoring work balances in certain markets or to ensure a business is staffed adequately. However, you would have to provide substantial benefits and added compensation to those who are asked to relocate as it may require moving their family members.

Succession Planning

You need to look at what might happen when people are going to replace others in certain positions over time. Your plan for succession could include:

1. Review the high-risk positions that may require a succession process. The high-risk positions are ones that might include people retiring soon or people who might be likely to go elsewhere.

2. Review the functions and tasks of the high-risk positions.

3. Determine when those positions are going to be vacated.

4. Identify the requirements for other employees to move into vacated positions.

5. Perform a gap analysis to review the tasks required of the vacated positions.

6. Decide on developmental opportunities of employees already on staff.

7. Develop a candidate pool. The pool may be internal candidates as well as people who may be hired from outside.

Employee Relations

You need to consider the rights that you and your employees have according to law.

Job Contract

The job contract has to include a job description and a statement of authority. Performance requirements surrounding what one needs to be should be listed. Details on the proper compensation involved may also be handled here. You can also discuss benefits and other things in the contract as well as details about when a person may be terminated from a position.

An oral contract may not be valid.

Managing a Relationship

You can use a few strategies for managing relationships with your employees. HR can start by reviewing the union rules of the employees who belong to a union. You need to identify the terms of any unions that might work at your property if you have any.

You can produce an employee recognition plan that considers how and when certain rewards are to be given.

Governmental rules about labor limits, safety standards, and other details should be noted.

Collective Bargaining

Collective bargaining is a practice to manage contracts with workers. Collective bargaining focuses on negotiating deals with workers, unions, and other entities. The practice requires you to prepare for the negotiations and to determine the needs of the company and the other parties.

The HR department must review the collective bargaining based on the expenses associated with the terms. A schedule for negotiations needs to be created.

Administering the Contract

The administration process for the contract following collective bargaining depends on the agreements between the company and the unions. A memorandum of understanding (MOU) must be developed to explain the details of the bargained contract. This will detail how grievances are to be resolved.

Handling Grievances

Grievances are issues people have regarding complaints surrounding the work environment. Many grievances that an HR department will handle will be problems relating to how work shifts are assigned, the hours of work, or how certain benefits that a person is entitled to might not be being provided.

The process of handling a grievance often begins with a written complaint. The complaint will explain in detail the problem that a worker has. The discussion between supervisors about the grievance should be documented. A managerial discussion can be planned to identify what must be done. Proper mediation or arbitration may be held to agree on the solution for the problem.

Resolving Conflicts

There are times when a relationship between a worker and the employer may be fractured. Much of this may be problems surrounding training, compensation, work duties, or even personal issues that might be hindering the worker.

To resolve a conflict, you must seek to understand the concern that the employee has and show that you are willing to resolve the problems.

Mediation and Arbitration

Mediation and arbitration may be necessary if you need a third-party to help you with the process. These practices keep issues from moving to a court.

1. Mediation

Mediation is a process where the parties in the dispute actively participate. The parties will establish a meeting with an independent counsel who attempts to find a solution. The process is mutual and ensures the two sides are satisfied with the end result.

2. Arbitration

Arbitration is a formal procedure that is handled by attorneys on each side. There is no private communication involved as the arbitrator will find a solution based on legal concepts and ethics. The process is to ensure a fair result based on legal considerations. One party may not win in the process.

Discipline

You may need to start disciplinary action against your employees if they are not following the company's standards. You may issue one of many warnings including oral or written warnings. A written warning should indicate the seriousness of the issue.

A suspension may be necessary if a person does not correct their behavior. The length of the suspension may be determined based on the severity of the issue or how often a person has received warnings. A termination would occur if the employee's issues cannot be resolved and there is no foreseeable way that the employee is willing to comply.

Technology and Data

An HR department can use technology to confirm document signatures, provide online learning and training, keep records, and offer digital training and self-service portals for employees. Technology is intended to make efforts for managing data and content easier.

Big Data Use

Big Data usage can be vital for the evolution and advancement of the company. Data mining is used to help you find content and establish connections between different aspects of work and the functions of the business. Mapping can help you with making strategic reviews. It is recommended that you analyze the functionality of any Big Data you have and that you work with appropriate controls.

Information Systems

Your HR information system may be established with employee records at the start. These records should include details on their pay rates and job titles, contact information, original employment data, and a list of certifications.

An HR portal may allow employees access to specific information. An employee self-service or ESS site may be accessed through the HR portal and may allow employees to adjust certain things, such as their contributions, contact information, and/or schedules. A manager self-service or MSS site can also be accessed through the HR portal, but it would be used for reviewing job analysis, identifying disciplinary actions, or planning schedules for workers.

Implementing the HR Information System

Your HR team must review the requirements for the HRIS and consider the software for the HRIs technical requirements.

Management can decide it a continuous integration is appropriate or if implementing the changes all at once.

An Employee Handbook

An employee handbook includes all the things that people need to know about their employment and what they can and cannot do in the workplace. The handbook provides thorough details on policies in the workplace, general values for the work environment, procedures, benefits, and disciplinary rules.

BYOD Policy

A bring your own device or BYOD policy may be established in your workplace if you wish. The policy details rules for employees to bring particular devices for work purposes, for example, laptops, tablets, smartphones, and other devices. This includes using certain programs or apps. You need to ensure that there are rules about what people can and cannot do with their devices, even if this requires the use of firewalls that may block certain websites or activities from being accessible.

Social Media Rules

While it is fine for people to criticize their employers on social media, those people must not engage in acts of harassment toward various people in the workplace. People should avoid disclosing private or confidential information on social media as such actions may harm the company.

Chapter 5 – The Workplace

The workplace segment of the SHRM tests is a review of activities that may take place in your work environment. Much of this focuses on producing a diverse and supporting workforce while managing the risks that may develop. Being able to handle the well-being of all the people in the workplace and how they are supported is important.

HR in the Global Context

Globalization allows people to interact with one another on a larger scale than ever before. People are more in touch with each other for various reasons, including economic influences, a need for security in today's workforce, and the ability to reach more allies. In addition, many emerging economies around the world are growing, with many of these economies having younger workforces and have environments where innovations have yet to move forward.

Hyper-connectivity has become a major influence in today's workplaces. Unified forms of communication are prompting people to get together in more ways than ever before. The online world is dependent on communications facilitated in minutes or seconds that used to take days.

How Work Is Being Moved

Outsourcing often occurs where work is transferred to outside organizations while not impacting the employer's payroll. Off-shoring can involve some work being sent to sources outside the country to reduce costs. On-shoring involves processes being moved to low-cost locations inside one's own country. Near-shoring is business processes being contracted to a nearby country, like American processes being moved to Mexico or Canada.

A general review of a talent pool based on cultural differences and languages spoken is important including possible risk levels, sociopolitical influences, and ethical differences. A review of the costs of hiring people in different parts of the world and in managing tax structures has to be considered.

Push Factors

Global businesses are often impacted by what is known as push factors. These factors will directly influence a business to partake in global expansion. Such push factors include:

1. The domestic demand for certain products or services may be saturated, thus requiring a business to reach out to other markets.

2. There aren't enough resources in one's local area for business, thus a need to find resources elsewhere.

3. Trade agreements are being signed between competitors.

4. New technologies are making it easier for people to interact with each other, thus increasing business opportunities.

5. Production can be facilitated in many places around the world.

6. Added costs and domestic economic worries may become worries.

7. It may be easier for a business to enhance its image when it expands to a different part of the world.

Pull Factors

Pull factors are what may cause foreign markets to become more appealing. These might influence the possibility of a business to grow and move in a different market. Such pull factors are:

1. Government policies can influence what happens in the workplace.

2. Strategic controls being put in place.

3. Unique growth opportunities may be used, especially when it comes to fast-growing economies.

4. The barriers to trade and investments may also be declining in intensity.

Globalization

Globalization is a practice that makes a business more visible. A business will have to work with upstream or downstream plans to make this work. An upstream strategy for globalization is getting a workplace to be aligned with a centralized party working on a task. A downstream practice focuses on decisions being made locally by subsidiaries. As a result, one of the four strategies may be used to globalize a business:

1. Global – the world is one market, and the same standards work everywhere

2. International – products are released to select markets

3. Transnational – strong connections between many global markets to attempt to create unique local markets

4. Multi-domestic – the headquarters does not control remote subsidiaries

Perlmutter's Orientations

Howard Perlmutter states that many management solutions can be used in the workplace. The EPRG model is as follows:

1. Ethnocentric – People in an ethnocentric society believe their home countries are better than others. They want to find new markets similar to theirs. Few adaptations will be made on certain products or services.

2. Polycentric – All countries involved are unique in this situation.

3. Regioncentric – There are many differences and similarities in many parts of the world. Unique strategies are built around these changes.

4. Geocentric – The entire world is seen as one large market.

What an HR Department Does

The HR department will have to know what it takes for a business to grow with globalization in mind:

1. Shoring

Off-shoring is where production goes to another country and on-shoring is where processes are contracted to other groups in one's home country. Near-shoring involves processes being contracted to a place close to the company's home. Outsourcing is working with vendors that can handle services separate from the company. The latter uses call centers and shipping stations. An HR group must figure out what strategy will work best for the company.

2. Standards

An HR team should also review the standards and rules that the company has set. These include legal requirements and other standards to follow. A unique supply chain for talent should also be planned with distinct rules for employment.

3. The personality of your workplace.

You need to review how open your workplace is, how flexible it is, and whether the workforce is cohesive.

4. Culture of the country you are interacting with

All countries have distinct cultures: the Sinosphere or East Asian sphere, and the Arab, Tibetan, and Islamic cultures are each unique. Different cultures have different rules and regulations, different employment laws, standards for etiquette, and considerations relating to language and terms that may be used to communicate.

Planning Global Assignments

You will have to assess and select a suitable person for a global assignment. Then, you must look at any visa requirements or other standards that are needed to allow someone to enter and work in a particular part of the world. The person should be trained to understand the culture in which they will be working.

Diversity and Inclusion

Diversity is critical to growing a business. Diversity refers to how business has many viewpoints and groups that are different. Those who work in diverse environments are more likely to succeed because they are frequently challenged to work with different ideas and concepts in the workplace.

Inclusion considers people of diverse backgrounds given equal opportunity to succeed. The most important point is to ensure that you combine diversity and inclusion so all staff will be comfortable with their work. This includes ensuring that there are no biases involved. By allowing all to be heard, new ideas can be utilized while old ideas may be challenged or in other cases modified.

You will need to work with the many layers of diversity for success. These include layers based on personality, inside dimensions, outside factors, and organizational forms of work. Internal points may be hard to control, but outside factors may be resolved well. The culture in the workplace can also be controlled to ensure diversity and inclusion is supported.

The steps for planning a diverse and inclusive environment are:

1. Review the outside market.

You might have to consider the types of people in your area who might be hired and how they might contribute to your business.

2. Assess your work environment.

Review your work environment based on the infrastructure you have established for supporting people and for establishing diversity. You can communicate with many in the work environment and establish suitable strategic alliances to help you meet certain standards and rules for work.

3. Plan the appropriate changes.

The changes can include new recruitment or sourcing as well as specialized plans for hiring. You would also have to review different cultural standards for each new hire. Be aware of any promotional or compensation that you might include as an incentive.

4. Emotional intelligence of the people in the workplace.

The emotional intelligence in the work environment refers to how well people are able to handle work routines and concepts that can directly impact an employee or a group of employees. Determine how the people in the workplace are responding to your initiatives and if there is agreement.

5. Plan mentorship programs.

Mentorship encourages people to feel more comfortable with the activities in the workplace. Employees appreciate knowing that there are people who are available to help them with many of their tasks.

6. Engage in team-building activities.

One way to allow people to be inclusive is to support team-building activities where people can interact with those of different cultures. Such activities may help with making it easier for workers to feel confident with the efforts they are putting in and how they can move forward with their tasks at hand. The efforts here can be thorough and unique, but you must ensure that the work is being planned accordingly and that there is enough representation in the various groups you are working with here.

Risk Management

Risk refers to concerns that may develop in the work environment that might interfere with the company's progress. You may encounter preventable risks that can be avoided, but strategic risks that can be identified in a planning session must be noted as well. External risks that come from outside the business may play a role in the business and as such would be impossible to remove.

ISO 31000 states that you must review the risk criteria that might influence the work of your business. You have to analyze the goals and policies as well as the scope of the work in question. Any risk tolerances you have and the availability of information should be noted in particular.

You may also notice possible conflicts of interest in the workplace. Such conflicts might arise when people are unable to be impartial when planning a solution.

Managing risk in the workplace includes the following:

1. Identify the risks.

The risks should be examined through various methods, including through brainstorming, interviewing, reviewing root causes, or using a SWOT analysis. A Delphi technique uses anonymous experts from outside the workplace to analyze the problem without bias. Experts in your field may also be consulted, although this is most effective when they are anonymous.

2. Use a risk scorecard or matrix.

A scorecard or matrix will focus on how your business is managed. The contents of the scorecard or matrix can vary, but you must measure your concerns based on how significant certain risks are, the potential for them to influence your workplace, and how much damage would be done if those problems were not resolved.

You can use key risk indicators to determine the problems that the business might incur. You will need to identify these indicators and decide how intensive they might be.

3. Remove uncertainties.

You can identify uncertainties and how they may be defined to simplify the management process.

4. Review the ownership.

You may consider sharing duties, or you can transfer duties to others. You may also increase or decrease certain tasks without fully making other people the owners of the process.

5. Communicate with others in management.

You will have to communicate the issues with others and then illustrate certain solutions based on what you feel is appropriate for your business. You can also establish guidelines for certain tasks.

6. Test the processes involved.

Oversight can help identify how well your business is handling certain tasks. You can perform debriefs of any process to ensure that the risk management processes are sensible and controlled.

Corporate Social Responsibility

Corporate social responsibility or CSR refers to how a business operates ethically. This includes working with philanthropic, transparent, and sustainable efforts. Additionally, there is a need to support one's community environmentally. Your CSR efforts are going to be shaped by many parties including:

- Corporate governance

- The rights of your workers

- Diversity

- Social responsibility

- Stakeholder relationships

- How you conduct yourself in the community

- Ethics in the organization

- Data security

- The values and culture in your workplace

- Community relations

- Employee relations

You will have to focus on producing CSR standards that work with various frameworks and guidelines including rules surrounding Organization for Economic Cooperation and Development or OECD standards. This includes maintaining transparency in the workplace, environmental standards, and ensuring a business works in accordance with the needs of the target consumer groups.

Other aspects of CSR are the United Nations Global Compact principles about human rights and labor. This includes ensuring a business treats its workers fairly while avoiding abuses. The Caux Round Table Principles should also be reviewed based on the roles that a business can play in economic and social conditions. The principles include respecting stakeholders outside of shareholders, contributing to positive developments in one's community, and building trust with the public while respecting the rules and being responsible.

ISO 26000 particularly states that CSR efforts should involve social responsibility including managing human rights concerns and handling labor practices and environmental standards correctly. Consumer issues and fair operating practices should be considered to follow standards.

In terms of philanthropy, your business should consider making efforts to help people who are relevant to your business. This includes working on initiatives that relate to the people who are your target audience. For instance, a fashion retailer that focuses on women could offer philanthropic help for organizations dedicated to research in breast cancer. Volunteering at charitable events can also be considered, although this would be without any pay for employees who work at such volunteering events.

Employment Law and Regulations (in the United States)

Be aware of the laws and regulations and court standards in the state you are conducting business.

Personnel Files

You will need to ensure that you have appropriate personnel files on hand to record details on each of the employees in your workplace. A personnel file will require the following:

1. Application details – These are reports and verification documents.

2. Payroll info – Details on any W-4 forms, weekly time sheets, and attendance record reports.

3. Performance reports – Progress reports and other details on how people are behaving and functioning in the workplace.

4. Training – Details of any training programs that have been completed by the employee.

5. Benefits – Details on health and other benefits that the employee has been assigned.

Your personnel files should NOT include medical records, investigation records, security clearance details, or any marginal files. These items should be kept confidential and private and must be separate from the personnel file.

Chapter 6 – Planning and Managing a Strategy

Strategy for planning refers to understanding how you will manage a project and how systems work. You have to describe a mission for your workplace and plan a project accordingly. This includes knowing how you're going to manage your strategies and how you will define the company's goals.

As a human resources professional, you will have to know how your business units are going to manage the strategies that are necessary including workforce planning the talent in your workplace that is available. You could also consider general incentive compensation and programs that will be initiated, as well as how your employees are going to adapt to the plans and strategies.

Main Goals

1. Consider the business decisions you wish to make. You need to prepare a plan based on the goals you have set. Senior HR professionals should talk with other business leaders regarding different strategies to use.

2. Action plans must be set up based on your HR strategy and how you're going to make changes within your business.

3. Benchmarks and metrics should be analyzed to determine the general competitive advantages that your company has.

4. A senior leader will have to develop strategies that align with certain goals.

You must align your effort and control the drift that might develop. Review the core competencies of what works.

Three Levels of Planning

You're going to work with three distinct levels of planning when getting your strategy ready:

1. Organizational

The organization level of planning is a review of what may happen in the future. A full analysis of what you are doing in the work environment should be planned based on what is appropriate and how you're going to implement changes. You can use the organizational effort to help you determine what might be useful in the situation and how you're going to keep the work functional.

2. Business Unit

There might be certain divisions or regions in your workplace to determine who is going to work on particular tasks.

3. Operational

You can plan strategies based on marketing, financing, manufacturing, and merchandising among other factors. You can use many of these operational-level strategies for making your work run efficiently and have the best results.

The Value Chain

The chain refers to a process of soliciting ideas or other assets and adds value to them through various functions. The process is to create unique ideas or concepts that add extra value to people. The ideas being produced work best when they are conveyed to the customers.

Your value chain may include several primary concepts. These include details about how inbound materials are arriving, the operations in the workplace, and any service feature that your employees provide. The primary concepts are essentially the things that a business has direct control over.

Secondary concepts will directly influence how the primary features operate. Having enough support for the secondary features will keep your business active and functional. The organizational structure has to be secure and sensible. Talent management should be considered to manage the people involved. You also have to identify various opportunities for research and development.

The Stakeholder

One thing to notice when developing your strategy for HR is to look at the stakeholders. You can look at how many people are going to contribute to the organization. The people who are stakeholders will be involved with the organization like owners and employees. The customers and the local community will play a role based on how they respond to what the organization might do. Outside pressure may also be produced by stakeholders such as the media, environmentalists, consumer advocates, special interest groups, and your local or national government. Any suppliers that you have will play a part too. Don't forget about your competition as the people who are challenging you might try to directly influence your decisions.

Developing a Strategy

It is time to consider the four steps to plan your strategy for HR. These steps are deciding on a strategy, developing that strategy, implementing the work, and reviewing how well effective the strategy was for the operation of the business. You will have to form your strategy by reviewing the information available to you. You can use primary research by directly looking for data and content on your own. You can also use secondary research based on what you feel is appropriate. You can use a smart plan to track and monitor what is happening in your work environment, thus giving you extra control over the process. You have to know how you're going to scan the environment and use the content in that environment to your advantage.

PESTEL Analysis

One option to develop a strategy is to use the PESTEL analysis. The analysis requires you to analyze your work based on six points:

1. Political

Political factors can be governmental policies and legal actions, any legislation that affects your business, and any rules might influence how your business operates.

2. Economic

Economic factors include everything from how you're doing business to the profitability of your business.

3. Social

Social factors relate to the beliefs and thoughts that people have. These include considerations of the population that is being supported and how these groups are going to handle different activities. You can use social factors to identify why people make decisions and what they may do in the future to make your business more viable.

4. Technological

Technology influences many functions including how to produce goods or distribute them. Methods of communication may also be considered.

5. Environmental

Environmental changes have become critical due to the raw materials available in many situations. Governmental regulations on how such materials are used have been changing. The expenses associated with using these materials should be considered.

6. Legal

Legal factors in your workplace include concerns surrounding the laws and rights that people have. An HR expert has to understand the concerns that might develop and find ways to resolve problems before they become an issue.

SWOT Analysis

Another part of producing a strategy is using a SWOT analysis. With this, you are working with the external and internal factors that might influence operations. The first two points in the SWOT analysis are internal, while the other two focus on what is outside your business:

1. Strengths – things that a business does well

2. Weaknesses – concerns for the business over what it does or things that need to be improved

3. Opportunities – things that could change in the future for a business to grow and be more successful

4. Threats – anything outside a business that might make it harder for the business to grow

Lifecycle Review

The lifecycle is the amount of time involved for some aspect of the operation to work well and to be positive. The lifecycle can be:

1. Introduction – something is new or unique ideas are generated

2. Growth – an organization is moving forward and growing

3. Maturity – the organization is at its maximum size to remain viable

4. Decline – outside advances and changes are making it harder for the business to stay afloat

Porter's Five Forces

The Five Forces produced by Michael Porter state that there are many pressures that could affect your business, such as:

1. New entries

There are times when new entries might get in the way of your business. When you are successful, you can expect other people to appear to compete with you. They might have different ideas of what should be done in your industry. The threat can make it harder for you to get the best possible profits.

2. Substitutes

There may be substitutes for what you are offering that will compete against you. These include products that are like yours but have some distinct differences that someone wants to market. In certain cases, the substitutes to your products can include knock-off versions of what you have provided or your patent is absent or has expired.

3. Bargaining Power of Customers

A customer can cause changes in the price of a product. This includes causing the cost of something to decrease dramatically. Some large-scale retailers might attempt to change the values of things because they are making those products more accessible to a greater number of people.

4. Bargaining Power of Suppliers

A supplier might not have many options for you to consider when it comes to the parts and other items you wish to use. They may keep the prices high because there is competition for their product.

5. Rivalries

Rivalries in your industry happen when people are competing and they offer products for less or try to make their product more appealing to mainstream audiences. Such rivalries can entail intense competition and can be frustrating.

Growth-Share Matrix

A growth-share matrix is a review of the market share versus market growth. Any cases where there is a low market share and market growth rate might suggest that something has to be abandoned. Anything with a high share and low growth rate should indicate an opportunity for investment and for potential profits.

Nine-Box Matrix

A nine-box matrix helps you identify how well something is working based on the attractiveness of the industry versus the competitive strength. You might find that something is intriguing if it is attractive and the strength of your unit is high. The opposite suggests that there are concerns surrounding the popularity of a product.

Determining Your Values

To start, you have to establish a mission statement that explains the purpose of your business. Also, a vision statement that explains the problems you want to solve and where you want your business to go should also be planned.

The values set for your business can include specific principles that you feel are appropriate. Anything surrounding the role of your business and how it's going to work should be noticed for the best results and to decide where you want your business to go.

SMART Goals

You can also establish SMART goals are designed based on what you feel is sensible or suitable for your work needs. The goals are defined based on five critical points:

1. Specific – A goal should be defined

2. Measurable – You have to know how to measure your goals

3. Attainable – Everything must be sensible

4. Realistic – The work must be relevant

5. Timed – A timeframe might help to attain your goal

Developing a Strategy

The process of developing a strategy is particularly critical for senior HR professionals. You will need to analyze several considerations including producing appealing strategies that allow you to compete in the marketplace.

There are several steps you may use when producing your strategy:

1. Review your business and decide how it may work.

2. Share the responsibility to identify the goals and plans for the business.

3. Review your human resource department as though it were a unique business.

4. Measure the outcomes and not the processes.

5. Consider how the people in your business will respond.

6. Determine statistics or other numbers that might explain how your business is to grow and thrive.

7. Technology and innovations can be included in your strategy.

Analyzing Your Growth Strategy

Several things can be done when working with your growth strategy. To start, you may consider penetrating a market to increase your reach, or expand into a market you have never entered before. You could also expand the variety of products or services that you wish to highlight. Diversification can be selling new products in new markets.

Here are five aspects of designing your work:

1. Review the vision.

Your vision is a look at the desired results of your HR strategy. Look at what you aspire to do and how you'll achieve it.

2. Consider the business mission.

A mission is an objective for what you wish to do. The objective has to be clear and understandable. You can use the mission as a guideline for where your business is going.

3. Review your goals.

You might have various goals that you want to achieve.

4. Consider your strategies.

You might have very specific strategies including an analysis of what might be appropriate for the business and if those strategies are useful in the long run.

5. Look at the initiatives that you want to use.

You have to look at tactical and operational initiatives to successfully implement strategies to meet the goals you have set.

Additional Points to Develop Your Strategy

1. Analyze how you will differentiate your work.

You can differentiate the work based on factors like product features, performances, conformity to standards, and how reliable or durable something may be. Service differentiation is how products are delivered and how service is provided.

Channel differentiation involves the expertise and knowledge involved with a certain field. Relationship differentiation would involve courtesy and reliability while being simple in operation. You can also look at differentiation based on your company's image or reputation and price differentiation.

2. Strategy based on Porter's concepts.

Porter states that there are many competitive strategies that you can use. The differentiation should entail how you're going to make your efforts unique. A focus may also look at the niche market that you want to highlight.

Porter argues that there is a need to determine how you're going to trim the costs of running your business. In some cases, this might involve getting a better market share by offering lower prices. In other cases, you might produce a business based on the very bare essentials.

3. Know when you need to continue or divest.

You might have a situation where you need to divest from what you are handling. Divestiture is the opposite of investing. You might need to consider breaking away from some of the HR strategies you're planning.

4. Communicate about the strategy.

You have to let people know what works for you while also keeping your message simple yet detailed. They need to know how things might change and understand the reasons behind the changes in strategy.

You could also explain changes to your customers. You can also explain your plans by working with new forms of media. You can use social media sites, blogs, and forums to get information out to the public and to your customers.

Implementing the Strategy

The implementation involves a strategy being converted into action. The implementation process will require an analysis of who is responsible for the work and how certain tasks are to be completed. Conduct regular reviews to monitor the progress being made.

Several things can be done to implement the strategy:

1. Determine the resources.

Decide how to manage your resources both in the workforce and the finances you have available.

2. Provide the executive summary.

The executive summary explains the resolution and what resources are necessary along with defining the implementation.

3. Gather any support documents, such as financial analysis, a review of HR impacts, any influences on the business, and any responsibility changes that might develop.

4. A Gantt chart to list details of the implementation process.

A Gantt chart is a listing of the tasks that have to be done for the implementation to be successful. The Gantt chart includes a timeframe on an X-axis with several categories of different tasks. The chart can be updated with new events or with realistic information based on when things are actually occurring. You might need to update the chart on occasion if you are ahead of schedule or behind schedule.

Making the Implementation Successful

The implementation process may involve a merger, acquisition, or reorganization in your workplace while ensuring the HR department is operational and active. The solutions that are encouraged for use by the Accelerating Implementation Methodology system are:

1. Review the changes in the workplace based on how the workers are behaving.

The changes can be judged effective depending on how the people in the workplace are responding to new actions. Sometimes the workforce might be receptive to the changes.

2. Choose a sponsor for your implementation.

A sponsor is someone who will sign off on your work. A sponsor could be a senior manager. The sponsor will be ready to help you with all your specific promotional routines to promote your business plans.

3. Review any resistance.

There's always the chance that some people will resist implementations that consist of changes. The disruptions that come with new projects might make it more difficult to get support from the workforce. Decide what you will do when confronted with resistance.

4. Keep communications open.

All communication should continue to inform the workforce about progress and disruptions and also to elicit feedback.

5. Arrange for reinforcements.

The reinforcements that you want to utilize should be planned accordingly. You can talk with many people in the workplace about what you're doing and how you want to move forward. You need to ensure the reinforcements that you're going to play will work accordingly. This could assist you well with figuring out where you might go surrounding your efforts.

Handling the Change

The changes that take place in your implementation process can often be difficult for some people to follow. People often prefer the status quo because they are familiar with it and aren't going to judge what might happen when things change and new things come about in the workplace or another environment one is in. You have to look at Donald Kirkpatrick's seven steps surrounding how the change in your workplace is to be managed:

1. You have to determine the need for change or if people want the change.

2. Prepare the plans for whatever change might come about.

3. Discuss any possible reactions that might come about.

4. A final decision should be made surrounding the change.

5. A unique plan should be made to where it's not hard to make the work run right.

6. The changes you want to plan out should be communicated well enough.

7. The change can then be implemented so it becomes easier for people to go forward.

These points are vital for allowing a change to go forward. However, you have to ensure that the work is managed well and that you're not making things more convoluted than necessary. For instance, you might come across concerns surrounding how well a task might work. People might be angry and would refuse to stick around with you. At the same time, some people may be highly enthusiastic about something and might want to try something of value at a time. You would have to notice the work you're planning to ensure you know where you're going.

Making the Changes Possible

You're going to need to ensure the changes that you plan are managed right and that you've got an idea of where you want to go with your work. You have to recognize the changes you want to plan and that you know where you're going with your work. The good news is that there are several things worth reviewing surrounding how you can make your changes possible. These are points based on what Ken and Scott Blanchard have come across:

1. Look at the ways how you're communicating ideas with people.

You have to explain to people what is happening and why something is working. The people who are working with you need to understand why you're doing things and where you want to go with the work you are planning here. People need to know why something is happening. They should also know where you're going with your work and what might happen.

2. Be personal in your approach.

Discuss the personal aspects that come with the work you're planning for others. Talk about the changes being made and what might work in any situation.

Explain why something is so valuable and helpful for all to follow. Let them know why a change is coming forward and what makes that change so valuable and essential. You'll need to look at how well you're going to make your efforts sensible.

3.   Figure out the action that you're going to work with.

You have to move forward with your work by looking at the unique action you want to utilize. This includes looking at how you'll plan your work if something does not go as planned or if there's a problem with your task at hand. You need to plan your actions based on what works the best for your routines and how you're going to go forward with them. Any changes to your organizational structure or the systems you're working with should be planned out as well.

4.   Promote the changes.

The implementation only works when people appreciate the change. You have to promote your changes based on what is working. Let people see what makes the changes special. Showcase whatever might be working at any moment. You need to get those people who are working for you to buy into whatever you are offering. This includes giving everyone a clear idea of what is working.

5.   Be collaborative in the work you're planning.

Collaboration is critical to your success in the workplace. You've got to allow for a strong sense of collaboration to ensure everyone in the workplace is comfortable with whatever is being done at a time. Explain to people what they can do to be involved and how they can help you out. Let people know what they can do so they will feel more invested in what you are offering. This lets those people feel confident in what you are doing while willing to agree with you on anything of value.

6.   Be ready to change some of your plans for future success.

The refinement process is critical for figuring out what can be done to improve upon what you are doing. You can refine your work functions as necessary and figure out ways to make your work a little better. This includes letting others know about why your work is so useful and helpful. You can explain to people why something is necessary, or what you might need to do to change things. After you figure out a few answers, you can refine your work to make the task at hand easier to support and organize. The goal is to make the change better than before.

Taking the Lead Role

SHRM also states that you should be using the LEAD standard when looking for ways to make your effort more visible. You can use the SHRM standard to help you with going forward and making the most out of your content. You can take the LEAD role when implementing a strategy by using three critical points:

1. Lead – Explain to people what makes something worth doing.

2. Educate – Train people to go along with your changes.

3. Advise – Establish a sense of transparency where everyone knows what is happening.

4. Demonstrate – Illustrate to people what makes certain tasks work.

Evaluating Your Strategy

The evaluation process identifies how a task has been completed and what needs to be done to make the tasks easier.

You'll have to evaluate the implementations based on the performance objectives that you set up earlier. These objectives should be simple enough so that everyone in the workplace is familiar with what has to be done and when. Keeping the expectations and plans clear is vital to the success of the project.

1. Detail your benchmarks.

Benchmarks describe what you want to accomplish. Making the most out of your benchmarks is vital for helping you to ensure you've got control of the project.

2. Invite people to be committed to your work.

Let everyone involved know what is planned. Explain the reasons they should agree with your plans.

3. Measure the progress.

The progress should be analyzed based on the plans and the time allotted for the completion of the work.

4. Provide feedback to everyone involved.

The feedback should be given to the workers as the job progresses.

5. Evaluate the effectiveness based on the results.

Metrics for Evaluation

Metrics help you to understand what is happening and if the implementation is effective.

1. Marketing metrics - how many people visit your website

2. Sales metrics

3. Financial metrics - your working capital or your cash flow

4. Social media metrics - various platforms you're using for promoting your business

5. Customer feedback metrics - survey responses or how often people return to your business

6. Employee metrics – employees who stay, the cost-per-hire, and the expenses associated with payroll and benefits

The interesting thing about these metrics is that not all of them are financial in nature.

The Analysis

The analysis effort you put into your work will help you identify many opportunities in your business. Analysis should include a review of trends, variance, and any regressions that occur. The analysis process can work with many resources to help you gather data including databases that you can use to store information for data mining purposes. The use of Big Data, or massive databases with an extensive array of elements involved, may be very useful.

A variance analysis involves a review of the difference between certain behaviors and what you might have planned at first. You can use the difference to determine if a strategy has excelled or fallen below your expectations.

Trend analysis is a review of business data based on many results and trends that become obvious. You might notice new ways people in the workplace are behaving. You might have to change strategies.

A regression could also be noticed and will identify possible causes and what needs to be done to resolve this condition.

Chapter 7 – Laws (United States)

The following are laws that will need to be followed if you are in the United States. These are laws that will vary based on the size of your company and how the organization works.

Note: This is not a fully comprehensive listing of the laws and court considerations that need to be followed. You can talk with a legal expert for additional details.

At Least One Employee

Clayton Act

The Clayton Act focuses on preventing mergers or other transactions that would limit competition. A single person cannot be a director of two or more competing entities.

Consumer Credit Protection Act

The CCPA states that there is a limit to the wages that can be garnished as a means of paying creditors. An employee cannot be fired due to garnishment.

Copyright Act

The Copyright Act states that an original work that has been copyrighted is protected so that another person cannot duplicate that work. General copyright can be in effect for the creator's life plus 70 years.

Electronic Communications Privacy Act

ECPA states rules surrounding how people can have access to information. Emails cannot be intercepted without one's permission according to ECPA. Any cases where people are to be monitored in the workplace must also be disclosed. People must agree to the surveillance; they cannot be monitored without their permission.

Employee Retirement Income Security Act

ERISA uses a series of standards about how employee benefit plans are to be established. Employees who have pension plans or other retirement packages should be allowed to redeem their money if their jobs are lost for any reason. A retirement plan must comply with IRS standards.

Fair Credit Reporting Act

The FCRA states that an employer must notify a person in writing if a credit report is required when making a decision on their employment. The person who will have one's credit profile monitored must agree to the action.

Fair Labor Standards Act

FLSA focuses on many protections for how people are to be treated. A minimum wage should be used alongside limits on how many hours a person should work in a week. Guaranteed time and a half may also be provided for overtime to people who work in particular jobs. Various records will be kept based on how an employee is paid, the hours worked each day, and when that person is to receive wages. Certain rules are applied regarding child labor and when minors can work.

Labor-Management Relations Act

The LMRA, or Taft-Hartley Act, prevents people from having to join a union in order to secure a job. This may be interpreted as unfair bargaining. In this case, people have the right to join or not join a union.

Labor-Management Reporting and Disclosure Act

Unions are given the right to secret elections and free speech rights. The Department of Labor requires annual financial reports.

Occupational Safety and Health Act

OSHA is a law that insists on a safe work environment. A company is to establish due diligence when taking care of people in the workplace. Proper warning systems and maintenance standards must be met. People should have access to proper safety equipment during the work process. Records on general safety standards in the workplace have to be kept as well.

OSHA states that on-site inspections can be conducted at any time. Any cases where people may be in imminent danger require people to be kept out of the workplace for an extended period to ensure no risks develop. All worker complaints about how the business is being run with safety in mind should also be reported as soon as possible to the OSHA, as these may entail violations.

Rehabilitation Act

The Rehabilitation Act states that people who are disabled have the right to be hired while working with vocational rehabilitation. This includes ensuring accommodation for those who are disabled and need extra help getting in and out of different areas in the workplace.

Sarbanes-Oxley Act

The Sarbanes-Oxley or SOX Act was designed in response to many financial scandals that caused significant economic damages during the turn of the 21st century. The Act states that corporate officers must be held liable for any financial discrepancies. Whistleblower protection must also be in effect.

Securities and Exchange Act

The Securities and Exchange Act focuses on a company that issues common stock for trade. A business must provide the appropriate disclosure. The Act also focuses on the operation of the Securities and Exchange Commission, a group that will identify the legal functions being handled in the workplace.

Sherman Anti-Trust Act

This particular law states that a business must not interfere with another business to cause damage. A business that attempts to restrict competition or fix prices may be punished. Restriction on trade is also prohibited.

Social Security Act

All people who pay taxes in the workplace should be taxed for Social Security payments. This is to support the Social Security system in the United States that helps those who are retired and those who are permanently disabled. This is to prevent poverty among those who are unable to work. Payroll deductions will be established via the SSA. The people who pay their Social Security taxes can receive their funds through the Social Security Administration after they retire or after they have become disabled for any reason.

15 or More Employees

Americans with Disabilities Act

The ADA states that people are not to be discriminated against because of any disabilities that they have including mental, physical, or developmental disabilities in all forms. An employer must ensure that any possible accommodations needed for that person are provided. This includes anything required for mobility, access, or general functionality. The key is to ensure that a person is capable of completing a job and that the appropriate accommodations are made. Anything that is provided must specifically be offered with professional use in mind and not necessarily as something from a personal standpoint.

The ADA also refers to the essential job functions so that the person expected to complete a job has the support from the employer to do the job properly.

However, job accommodations may not be required for all people. The accommodations should be reviewed if a person is struggling with certain actions and needs extra help.

Civil Rights Act (Title VII)

Title VII states that people are not to be discriminated against based on race, color, religion, sex, or national origin. A person cannot make a decision on employment based on any protected class.

Civil Rights Act (1991)

The 1991 amendment to Title VII states that an employee can demand a jury trial if they have been discriminated against due to their status of being a part of a protected group. There are limits as to how much money may be sought for damages.

Drug-Free Workplace Act

The DFWA ensures that appropriate drug tests are conducted upon employment. Random drug testing may also be required in some places, although the rules vary based on where the testing is taking place and the significance of the testing process. Records of drug tests must also be kept to ensure that a person can be identified as being safe to work with. This is based on the person not engaging in any activities that may be interpreted as being illegal.

Pregnancy Discrimination Act

The Pregnancy Discrimination Act states that pregnancy is a temporary disability. Therefore, job accommodation must be offered during the woman's pregnancy. The woman should also be given the right to her original job at the same pay rate after she returns following her pregnancy. A similar job may also be provided, but this must be as close to the original job as possible. The act is an extension of Title VII.

20 or More Employees

Age Discrimination in Employment Act

ADEA states that people who are over the age of 40 cannot be discriminated against in any way. A person who is found to have been discriminated against due to age will be reinstated and given any arrears or back pay that one might have missed due to the issue. Some exceptions may be found to the rule, although those exceptions are based more on individual industries. These include the aviation industry, which states that airline pilots who operate commercial planes must retire at the age of 65.

Consolidated Omnibus Budget Reconciliation Act

COBRA is applicable to businesses that provide group health insurance policies. An employee who is terminated can be provided the opportunity to continue to receive health benefits for a time provided proper contributions are made to the program during one's lifetime with the company.

50 to 100 Employees

Affirmative Action (Executive Order 11246)

Affirmative action means that equal employment opportunities must be provided to all persons. This includes ensuring that anyone can be allowed to get into a protected class regardless of one's status. Although this does not mean that quotas have to be used based on the types of protected classes people are in, you may still work with ensuring these groups are available for hire and that they are protected during the employment process.

Family and Medical Leave Act

The Family and Medical Leave Act focuses on various benefits for employees. Leave can be for up to 12 weeks in a 12-month period. The leave is unpaid unless the employer has a policy that states that a person will be paid. The 12-month period starts when the leave begins. The 12-week period can also be in increments of one day in many situations, thus allowing a person to spread the leave out. This applies to employees who have been working for the employer for at least a year.

A leave may cover childbirth or adoption, to care for ill persons in the family, or to manage one's own illness if the concern becomes significant. A 26-week period can also be granted to employees who are dealing with military duty-related injuries or illnesses. This includes cases where a family member might be experiencing a military duty-related issue.

More than 100 Employees

Worker Adjustment and Retraining Notification Act

The WARN Act states that an employer must be ready to help experienced employees to re-enter the workforce if one loses their job. The WARN Act states that a business must inform the workers 60 days in advance or greater when a place is closing or layoffs are to take place. This is to ensure that people are going to have enough time to find new employment. WARN does not apply if the layoff is going to be six months or less if fewer than 50 people are to be laid off.

Employment Visa Rules

Employment visas may be considered in the process of hiring employees from outside the country. These employment visa rules are relevant to American workplaces and must be adhered to.

An Employment non-immigrant visa may be issued to certain parties. An E-1 treaty trader visa applies to a person being employed through a treaty being made with another country. The person must depart the United States when the training process is completed. An E-2 treaty visa may be granted to someone who is personally invested in the enterprise. The investment that the E-2 visa participant has should be significant.

H visas are for those people who have met particular talent or educational requirements of the posted job. An H1-B visa requires a person to have a Degree in a particular field for that person to be able to work in a certain industry. An H1-C visa is for registered nurses working in professional areas where there is a healthcare shortage.

H-2A visas are for temporary agriculture workers. These include people who are doing temporary seasonal work. H-2B temporary visas are for non-agriculture workers. There must be proof that a person's work will be temporary. More importantly, the H-2B visa applies only when a person confirms that the work is not going to negatively impact the work of American employees who are employed to work in similar positions.

SHRM-CP Exam 1

1. A trainer is reviewing how well a training activity was received by the people in the workplace. What form of training analysis is that person using?
   a. Reaction
   b. Behavior
   c. Results
   d. Learning

2. A person's general knowledge and skills for work can be interpreted as:
   a. Return on investment
   b. Human capital
   c. Economic functionality
   d. Stress response

3. Joseph wants to receive a specific benefit at retirement. Jim has his employer match his regular contributions for use in retirement. What makes Jim's retirement plan different?
   a. He uses a contribution plan
   b. His retirement plan isn't defined
   c. He knows what benefits he holds
   d. He is getting the money sooner

4. Which of the following in the workplace could be interpreted as a "perk?"
   a. Compensation
   b. Perquisite
   c. Benefit
   d. Incentive

5. Social Security can be provided to American workers as:
   a. Compensation
   b. Prerequisite
   c. Benefit
   d. Incentive

6. What makes outsourcing different from off-shoring?
   a. Outsourcing is about transferring work sources outside the country
   b. Outsourcing entails moving work to groups outside one's payroll
   c. Off-shoring entails moving part of a business to an external company in a nearby country
   d. A and B

7. Some alternatives should be prepared when a strategy is developed for promoting HR actions. How many alternative options should be included at least?
   a. 3
   b. 4
   c. 5
   d. 6

8. The Drug-Free Workplace Act states that an HR firm needs to provide the following to employees:
   a. Details on counseling or rehabilitation programs
   b. Penalties for drug violations
   c. Details on the dangers of certain drugs
   d. All of the above

9. The Lilly Ledbetter Act is a law for HR groups to follow regarding:
   a. Fair pay
   b. Discrimination from sex
   c. Pregnancy discrimination
   d. Employee selection rules

10. Geographic differential pay may be offered when:
   a. People are expected to work longer in certain parts of the country
   b. It costs more to access a work site in certain areas
   c. Taxes are different in one place
   d. All of the above

11. Which of these makes the person considered a stakeholder?
    a. The person is a spouse of someone involved with the company
    b. The person has some investment in the company
    c. The person regularly shops at the store
    d. The person regularly reads advertisements for the store

12. What aspect of your HR work is not likely to be outsourced?
    a. Resource planning
    b. Payroll review
    c. Unemployment insurance
    d. Workers compensation claims

13. An identified risk in an enterprise may be called a:
    a. Key risk indicator
    b. Analysis fault
    c. Danger condition
    d. Barrier to entry

14. What should be done after you train your employees on how they are to handle risks in the workplace?
    a. Select the largest concerns of value
    b. Review plans for evolving and changing the work
    c. Create a framework for the operation
    d. Assign ownership to certain concerns

15. What can be done when aiming to resolve risks based on an enterprise risk management process?
    a. Produce an action plan
    b. Find ways to eliminate redundancy
    c. Review how you can avoid risks
    d. All of the above

16. Which of the following is not part of a SWOT analysis in business?
    a. Strengths of the organization and operations
    b. Outside threats to the business
    c. Workers Compensation

d. Opportunities for development

17. What should you review when analyzing the management in your workplace based on its functions?
    a. What a team does to avoid actions
    b. How it is capable of handling risks
    c. How different plans are resolved
    d. Knowing how people may use software programs of value

18. What defines a person-based pay system?
    a. Pay based on performance
    b. Pay from seniority
    c. Pay for how well a person can work based on competency
    d. Pay through a salary structure

19. A structural change is:
    a. A slight procedural alteration
    b. A new manager coming in
    c. Certain jobs being removed
    d. A change in the hierarchy in the workplace

20. A business that is interpreted as floundering has the following concern:
    a. It is unable to pivot
    b. It is not aware of the situation
    c. The entity can disrupt others
    d. The entity has been disrupted

21. A business that is aware of its situation and can pivot is known as a:
    a. Ponderer
    b. Survivor
    c. Loss Leader
    d. Nimble Entity

22. Roger Green states that disruption is not an event, but is a process that:
    a. Can be avoided
    b. Is a certainty
    c. Should be managed
    d. Is impossible to recover from

23. The MBO process entails all but which one of these steps?
    a. Monitor performance
    b. Reward the performer
    c. Review competitors
    d. Set goals

24. The goals in an MBO should be set based on:
    a. Difficulty
    b. Variety
    c. Flexibility
    d. A and C

25. What works best when establishing a competitive advantage?
    a. Technology
    b. Human capital
    c. Innovative ideas
    d. Customer quality

26. An employee handbook may be provided to workers when they start working for you. The handbook helps to:
    a. Establish expectations
    b. Provide legal details on the employment
    c. Works to keep the employer from being liable for certain problems
    d. Prepare a philosophy for work

27. What makes Medicare different from Medicaid?
    a. Income considerations
    b. Age rules
    c. Limits for use

d. All of the above

28. Is Medicaid capable of covering long-term care services?
    a. Yes, in all cases
    b. Yes, if they are considered necessary
    c. Yes, but only for a limited time
    d. No, in all cases

29. When can FMLA leave be used?
    a. When a person cares for a former spouse
    b. To care for an in-law
    c. To care for a 21-year-old child
    d. To care for grandchildren

30. What can be done for a vacation leave program to make it more valuable?
    a. Produce leave dates
    b. Add vacation time
    c. Reduce the advance notice requirement
    d. Assign leave based on different parameters

31. What makes arbitration and mediation alike?
    a. The processes are both non-binding
    b. A third-party helps
    c. Majority vote makes the decisions
    d. Persuasion is the key to resolving problems

32. What would Maslow consider to be a form of security for workers in an environment?
    a. Teamwork
    b. Job security
    c. Recognition
    d. Training

33. Which of the following things cannot   be said about unemployment benefits?
    a. Available to those on furlough
    b. Paid for up to 26 weeks unless there are high unemployment rates
    c. People who are fired for poor performance can get benefits
    d. Benefits are taxed on a federal level

34. Who would not be eligible for employment at will policy?
    a. Supervisor
    b. Veteran
    c. Disabled employee
    d. Bargaining unit worker

35. OSHA states that the work environment cannot be louder than this number of decibels or the conditions may be hazardous:
    a. 70
    b. 75
    c. 80
    d. 85

36. Which of the following is a central tendency measure?
    a. Ratio
    b. Mean
    c. Range
    d. Frequency

37. What would you do when instigating a performance management system in your work environment?
    a. To manage a person's development
    b. To figure out what contributions a person is making to a work environment
    c. To see how effective the employees in the workplace are
    d. To review how well the goals in the workplace are being determined or aligned

38. You can design a pay structure for the workplace based on:
    a. Job evaluation
    b. Market rates
    c. How often work is done
    d. A and B

39. The new pay structure in your workplace may be implemented based on:
    a. Roles
    b. Levels of experience
    c. How well a person tests
    d. All of the above

40. Which pay structure is based on a few broad salary ranges that will encourage an employee to develop skills while still keeping a promotion from being likely?
    a. Hays structure
    b. Pay classification
    c. Flex pay
    d. Broadbanding

41. What should you do when starting your training program?
    a. Determine if the training is necessary
    b. Establish a trial
    c. Figure out your objectives
    d. Get support from your higher-ups

42. This disparate action occurs when a person continues to hire people of a certain age or gender for the same type of job:
    a. Impact
    b. Treatment
    c. Discrimination
    d. Change

43. The most unique part of the Delphi method for creating answers is:
    a. You can get new employees to work with this
    b. The key entails asking as many new questions in the effort as possible
    c. This can work with as many or as few people as you wish
    d. It is a group of experts hired to find answers

44. The facilitator in a group session:
    a. Compiles responses
    b. Analyzes feedback
    c. Plans new routines
    d. Figures out the strategies that may work in a design effort

45. Short-term disability is:
    a. Federally regulated
    b. Part of a private plan
    c. Designed with unpaid leave
    d. Made without paperwork

46. Can you use the FMLA leave consecutively or intermittently?
    a. Consecutively
    b. Intermittently
    c. Both
    d. Your manager will make the decision

47. What is the time limit for rest and recuperation of the FMLA for military leave?
    a. 3 days
    b. 5 days
    c. 7 days
    d. 14 days

48. A rolling 12-month period in a benefit in your contract is work for:
    a. A calendar year
    b. A 12-month period from the date of an event
    c. Any 12-month period
    d. A 12-month period when something begins

49. Which is not one of the barriers listed in the Glass Ceiling Act of 1991?
    a. Governmental
    b. Internal
    c. Economic
    d. Social

50. Can a fee for service or FFS plan be interpreted as a health care plan?
    a. Yes, in all situations
    b. This varies based on what the FFS covers
    c. No, in all situations
    d. No, it is not offered by a worker

51. Gossip is a response to change that may occur and is considered:
    a. Uncertainty
    b. Judgments
    c. Refusal to work
    d. Hard feelings

52. What can be done first when implementing performance management in the workplace?
    a. Invite a commitment
    b. Set expectations
    c. Link to consequences
    d. Measure progress

53. All of these are negative habits determined by Marshall Goldsmith's analysis of how a business operates except:
    a. Passing judgment
    b. Playing favorites
    c. Making excuses
    d. Creative alternative mindsets

54. A leader may be likely to delegate tasks and not engage in many of these tasks on one's own. This could indicate a leader is a:
    a. Delegator
    b. Participant
    c. Seller
    d. Teller

55. A transformational leader is intended to be:
    a. Charismatic
    b. Stimulating
    c. Inspirational
    d. Relaxed

56. Skinner states that extinction occurs when this happens to an event:
    a. Surprise
    b. A desire to do something
    c. Not feeling any fear
    d. No response

57. A halo error in the performance appraisal process is:
    a. The employee is rated low in all errors
    b. The employee is rated high in all errors
    c. A bias influencing many results
    d. The most recent reports being favored above all else

58. An employment contract should review:
    a. Performance requirements
    b. Length of the agreement
    c. Job description
    d. All of the above

59. What is the greatest concern surrounding an oral contract in employment?
    a. The content in the contract may be false
    b. The details are not thorough
    c. The content may be unofficial
    d. The wrong person might be conveying the information

60. A buyout would be used when terminating a person who:
    a. Has engaged in illegal activities
    b. Has time left on one's work contract
    c. Has unused vacation pay
    d. None of the above

61. A company car is an example of a:
    a. Perk
    b. Benefit
    c. Compensation
    d. Performance reward

62. Which is the first step to follow in the contract negotiation process?
    a. Prepare
    b. Open
    c. Argue
    d. Explore

63. What is involved in the communication for arbitration?
    a. Private meetings can be conducted with an arbitrator
    b. The meetings are joint
    c. No private communication with the arbitrator
    d. No attorneys are needed

64. What is the goal of the mediation process?
    a. A mutual agreement
    b. One side has to clearly win
    c. The project in question could be deferred
    d. A new alternative may be the solution

65. A business in the United States that engages in near-shoring could move a process to:
    a. Iceland
    b. Canada
    c. Portugal
    d. China

66. What will influence your ability to interact well with a different culture?
    a. Flexibility
    b. Openness
    c. Social dexterity
    d. All of the above

67. The Indosphere is an aspect of culture that covers:
    a. East Asia
    b. Southern Asia
    c. China
    d. Indonesia

68. An elite corporate culture can be distinguished by how the company would:
    a. Attempt to grow fast
    b. Allow for collaboration
    c. Use a specific hierarchy
    d. Consider progressive activities for development or evolution

69. Which is an example of primary research?
    a. Trend review
    b. Academic journal
    c. Published book
    d. Interviews you conduct

70. A matrix organization will have how many managers?
    a. 1
    b. 2
    c. 3
    d. 4

71. A supervisor who aims to establish cooperation is using this form of leadership:
    a. Transformational
    b. Democratic
    c. Authoritarian
    d. Transactional

72. What is not included in the ADDIE model?
    a. Design
    b. Implement
    c. Direct
    d. Analysis

73. The implementation step in the ADDIE model should include:
    a. Seeing if the tools in the workplace are ready to use
    b. Reviewing how prototypes are working
    c. Planning a pilot session
    d. The development of the course materials

74. Is the federal or state minimum wage applicable to the workplace?
    a. Federal wage
    b. State wage
    c. Whatever is larger
    d. Whatever is smaller

75. What makes a public domain rule different from fair use?
    a. Public domain works are cheaper
    b. Public domain works can be owned privately
    c. Critical reasoning is vital for identifying certain terms
    d. Public domains are available to the public

76. Fair use rules can be reviewed based on:
    a. Factor
    b. Value
    c. Purpose
    d. Level of exposure

77. Which of the following is one of the four Ps of marketing?
    a. Product
    b. Planning
    c. Persistence
    d. Penetration

78. What can make it difficult to promote a rewards package in the workplace?
    a. High turnover
    b. Struggles to get new talent
    c. Attempting to be visible in a new field of endeavor
    d. High sales

79. A small business that aligns with other small businesses to establish a combined plan will participate in:
    a. Health purchasing alliance
    b. Partially self-funded plan
    c. Administration plan
    d. Service-only plan

80. People who are referred to a temp agency to work somewhere may be subjected to:
    a. In-house hiring
    b. On-call hiring
    c. Temp-to-perm hiring
    d. Payrolling

81. Which of the following is not an international risk surrounding organizational efforts?
    a. Customs
    b. Laws
    c. Languages
    d. Production values

82. What should be included in an employee's separation file?
    a. Reports on severance
    b. The rationale for removing someone
    c. Exit interview form
    d. Details on what one earned

83. What medical records can you keep about an employee?
    a. Diagnostic records
    b. Drug test records
    c. Lab test results
    d. All of the above

84. What can you do regarding a person's criminal record when reviewing if someone is to be provided security clearance?
    a. See if a person has worked for legal authorities
    b. See if a person has been fined
    c. Review one's arrest record
    d. Analyze any possible bargaining efforts

85. What should you do according to the law when a record has expired?
    a. Save it in a secure file
    b. Destroy it
    c. Give it to the person that the record is for
    d. Add to a different record for the same person

86. Diaspora refers to:
    a. People forced to leave their homeland
    b. People traveling outside their home countries to work
    c. People wanting to collectively enhance their skills
    d. A medical illness that requires short-term disability coverage

87. What should be done when sending a worker on an international assignment?
    a. Review the support for the employee at the new location
    b. Provide help with language issues
    c. Offer publicity
    d. Provide anything a worker needs before landing in a different location

88. Diversity and inclusion need to be considered for:
    a. People of color
    b. Large companies
    c. All organizations
    d. People who have complaints that need to be resolved

89. The main goal of an inclusion program is to:
    a. Ensure all people can contribute to the workforce
    b. To get a business to work with quotas
    c. To diversify the business
    d. To analyze how well a business is organized based on its functionality

90. An employee affinity will include:
    a. Rules for hiring more people in one group
    b. Enticing other employees to form unique groups for defense purposes
    c. To review changes to diversity programs as they are needed
    d. To figure out what languages are to be spoken in the workplace

91. A risk register is a record of:
    a. Identified risks
    b. Insurance costs
    c. Repair bills in the workplace
    d. How well computers are working in the office

92. Social responsibility pertains to all but one of the following:
    a. Communications with others
    b. Human rights
    c. Environmental controls
    d. Fair operations

93. Environmental efforts in the workplace must entail preventing pollution. Part of this may entail:
    a. Reducing emissions
    b. Producing transportation limits
    c. Establishing rules for how people can bring resources to the workplace
    d. Managing paper usage

94. The integration process for running different social responsibility standards in the workplace may include rules surrounding:
    a. Cost-effective measures
    b. Etiquette rules
    c. Complex procedures
    d. Normal and acceptable behaviors

95. The reporting process must entail content for reports being handled:
    a. Accurately
    b. Quickly
    c. To the right people
    d. A and B

Answers to SHRM-CP Exam 1

1. a. The trainer is using a reaction plan to determine what is happening based on how people act and what might occur.

2. b. Human capital refers to the general skills and knowledge that one has for managing certain tasks.

3. a. Jim is using a contribution plan that entails him giving money to his program now with the intention of getting more money in the future.

4. b. A prerequisite is something discretionary in nature. This could be access to a company car or an in-store discount.

5. c. A benefit is something that is special compensation for certain actions. This includes non-wage compensation.

6. b. This is outsourcing, a practice where the other entity helping is outside one's payroll.

7. b. You need at least four alternative options with different cost, schedule, and risks involved with each one.

8. d. People in the workplace have to be fully aware of the risks involved with drugs. The DFWA requires an HR firm to inform people about the dangers of drugs and what can happen regarding their jobs if they are actively using drugs.

9. a. The Ledbetter Act of 2009 states that people should be paid the same for doing the same job based on experience and not on gender or other demographic points.

10. b. A geographic differential pay plan works when a person's environment or other travel needs make it harder to do the job.

11. b. Stakeholders are people who have an interest in the business in question.

12. a. Resource planning is identifying current goals for work and what is needed for attaining results. It would be difficult or impractical for this segment of the work to be outsourced.

13. a. A key risk indicator is an issue that will suggest there is a problem that may develop in the workplace.

14. d. You can assign ownership of key risk indicators to certain people in the workplace and then plan reviews based on how those people are capable of handling them.

15. d. The risk alleviation process should include consideration of how you will manage a plan for handling risks while also noting how those risks can be prevented. You can reduce the redundancy in the workplace as well to keep errors and other issues from developing depending on the situation.

16. c. The SWOT analysis is used by an organization to identify strengths, weaknesses, opportunities, and threats related to business competition. Workers Compensation is not part of the analysis.

17. b. The capability of the management should be analyzed alongside how particular risks that are influential in the workplace.

18. c. The structure focuses on how competent a worker is and how that person might advance.

19. d. The hierarchy may change based on the types of positions that are included, not necessarily based on the specific people who are responsible for handling those positions.

20. b. A floundering business can pivot and therefore not be easily disrupted.

21. b. A survivor may also be interpreted as a disruptor due to the ability of the survivor to pivot and the ability to be aware of what is happening in the current environment.

22. c. This statement is one of Green's Laws of Disruption. A process has to be managed if a business is to survive complications or other disruptions.

23. c. The MBO cycle is setting objectives, setting specific objectives for employees, monitoring the performance, evaluating that said performance, and rewarding those who perform well.

24. a. Goals are to be established based on how well people can accept them, how difficult the goals are.

25. b. Human capital refers to the people in the workplace and the innovative ideas or actions they bring to the table. The human capital is necessary to ensure that a business can continue to grow and be more likely to succeed.

26. c. The handbook is designed to let employees know what they can and cannot do in the workplace. The employer has to produce clear instructions in the handbook to ensure that employees do not break any rules or possibly risk legal actions due to wrongdoings.

27. a. Medicaid is designed for people who have low incomes.

28. b. Nursing homes and assisting living centers are among the places that can be covered, although Medicaid applies only if there is confirmation that the housing is necessary for a person's life.

29. d. People are allowed to take leave when caring for a spouse, parents, children under the age of 18 that one is a legal guardian of, and any conditions of one's self.

30. c. By reducing the amount of advance notice a person needs, it is easier for an employee to reserve a time for being off work.

31. b. A third part is responsible for both situations. While arbitration is binding, mediation is non-binding and requires persuasion.

32. b. Job security provides a sense of continuity of the job for the employee.

33. c. Unemployment benefits are for those who have been fired for reasons that are outside of their control. A person who was fired for poor performance would be ineligible for such benefits.

34. d. Employment at will states that an employer can fire employees for reasons beyond their control. This is providing the reasoning is legal. No legal liabilities are to be imposed, although this may change when dealing with unionized workers.

35. d. OSHA states that a work environment is dangerous if the volume is regularly over 85 decibels. This is especially for environments where the volume is at 85 dB or greater on average during a typical eight-hour working day.

36. b. A central tendency measure is a review of the probability distribution. This may be interpreted as the center of measurement of other considerations. The mean, median, and mode are all central tendency measures.

37. d. The performance management system is a review of how well employees and others in the workplace can work to particular standards set by management.

38. d. A pay structure should be planned based on how well the job is handled. A review of the market rates can also help identify how well people are being paid by similar businesses.

39. d. You can pay people according to what they are doing and the value of the role in the workplace. A person's experience in a job is also a consideration of pay rate.

40. d. Broadbanding occurs when many pay grades are taken and combined to produce fewer grades with a wider variety of payments. This helps people

to develop their careers in certain positions without considering promotions later on.

41. a. There is a need to review how a business is working and the progress it is making.

42. b. Disparate treatment occurs when people are hired or not hired based on sex, race, and other factors. This is illegal in accordance with Title VII.

43. d. The Delphi method identifies a problem that must be resolved. The experts in the workplace will help you find an appropriate solution to the issue.

44. a. A facilitator can establish the process and determine the responses from the people responsible.

45. b. FMLA is a federal regulation. Short-term disability is covered by a private insurance plan.

46. c. You can use the 12 weeks of leave in the FMLA consecutively or intermittently.

47. b. The five-day period is to ensure that people in the military have enough time to get back to their routines after they are finished with certain military actions. This includes ensuring people are not forced back to work.

48. b. The FLMA states that the 12-month period beginning the date when a person first uses leave.

49. c. Economic is not a listed barrier. The other three are considered to be barriers that make it harder for women to attain major positions in their work environments.

50. c. The FFS plan is for many minor services and not for significant processes.

51. a. Uncertainty occurs when people are afraid of what might happen to a business in the future. Gossip can occur when people are unclear about what is happening and this can cause the spread of false information.

52. b. The SIMPLE practice states that you must set expectations and then invite a commitment.

53. d. Goldsmith states that a business needs to review fair practices and identify any possible faults that might develop. Part of this includes looking at how each person in the workplace is supported.

54. b. A participant leader is someone who is only observing what is happening. A delegator will relegate tasks but still engage in actions. The sellers and tellers are more active in the process, although the sellers are not going to delegate actions.

55. a. A transformational leader is someone who is willing to help people accept certain actions. This is different from transactional leaders who are more stimulating.

56. d. Extinction develops when the negative behaviors that one engages in causes a person to stop responding in some way.

57. b. The halo error occurs as one variable that is high-rated causes other variables to be high-rated even if they are not. The horn effect is the opposite - low-rated variables cause other variables to drop in value.

58. d. A contract is provided for a person to sign before starting a position. The contract will either be for the duration the person is employed or can be for a specific length of time.

59. a. An oral contract is not an official statement and is without documentation.

60. b. A buyout is when a person has a contract and the contract is being terminated before the expiry of the contract.

61. a. A perk does not necessarily have to be monetary but is rather a bonus that a person can use while employed.

62. a. The contract discussion should be initiated and prepared so that the two sides can argue over what is needed, and then explore ways to finalize the contract so that both sides agree with the conditions.

63. c. The arbitrator will only communicate with the attorneys.

64. a. Arbitration considers one side as the winner, mediation focuses on providing a compromise where both sides find agreement.

65. b. Near-shoring involves moving business functions to a place not far from the current location. In this situation, a business in the United States would move part of its business to Canada or Mexico.

66. d. Interactions with other countries require people to be open and accepting of ideas and being aware of the differences in certain cultures.

67. a. The Indosphere focuses mainly on India and various parts of East Asia like Sri Lanka and Pakistan.

68. a. An elite culture will want to develop innovative ideas and grow fast.

69. d. Primary research is work that you conduct on your own. Directly talking with others in interviews is an example of this.

70. b. The two managers in the matrix format are the product manager and the functional manager. These two parties are responsible for identifying many functions in the workplace.

71. a. A transformational leader is someone who works as a model and wants to encourage better relationships among all the people in the workplace.

72. c. The ADDIE model uses the steps: Analysis, Design, Develop, Implement, and Evaluate and not Direct.

73. a. The implementation stage is providing the training and to arrange for the necessary tools for the task. Observation is also necessary.

74. c. In accordance with FLSA standards, the higher wage is appropriate regardless of what the wage is at a federal or state level.

75. d. A public domain is something that is available for all and does not involve private ownership. The work is available for public use, although the rules may vary based on the country where you are operating.

76. c. Fair use is reviewing content based on nature, amount, purpose, and effect.

77. a. The four P's are product, place, promotion, and price. The product in this situation refers to the type of product being offered.

78. c. There may be struggles for a business as it aims to expand into a new field. A reward package may take some time to develop as the business enters a new field of work.

79. a. A health purchasing alliance is a situation where small businesses can band together to acquire a complete health service plan that may work for all of the employees in the same work environment.

80. d. Payrolling is a practice where temporary employees are hired by an agency and then sent to a business to work.

81. d. International risks include concerns surrounding laws, customs, and language.

82. c. An exit interview form includes details on the things a person might say about the company and the work that has been done while employed.

83. d. Records are critical for identifying different medical needs that a worker might have. These records can identify any tests that an employee failed.

84. c. The arrest record will determine why a person might have been subjected to criminal charges. You can use the details in the record to decide if you need to make certain changes to the terms of employment for that employee.

85. b. You must shred the documents that you have after their periods of usefulness have expired. This is due to the content being outdated and also sensitive.

86. a. In many cases, people who enter the workforce in one country are those who have been forced from their original home countries due to political pressure or persecution or due to armed conflicts.

87. a. Support should be provided to the people who are going to different countries to eliminate any confusion and uncertainties that they might have.

88. c. Diversity and inclusion ensure that all people in the workplace have a voice regardless of background.

89. a. Equality in the workforce is a critical part of what makes inclusion vital for a business to operate and function.

90. c. The changes involved in a diversity project may be based on religion, culture, ideology, and experience among other factors.

91. a. The risk register includes all risks that may develop in the workplace.

92. a. Social responsibility should be planned based on ISO 26000 standards. This includes looking at managing human rights, handling environmental concerns, working with fair operating processes, and lawful labor practices.

93. a. Emissions have to be controlled in the workplace to comply with the environmental standards in an area.

94. d. Social responsibility includes ensuring that proper standards of behavior are followed in the workplace.

95. a. Accuracy is critical for all reports.

SHRM-CP Situational Exam 1

1. A female worker is earning $500 a week doing a job, while a male worker doing the same job is earning $600 a week. The Equal Pay Act requires the employer to:
    a. Recruit at a higher pay rate
    b. Defend against possible discrimination
    c. Pay a differential for the female
    d. Use a banding system for male and female pay

2. Jeff recently had his work hours reduced due to a major reorganization campaign. What might influence the COBRA benefits that Jeff would earn?
    a. The fact that he did not leave his job altogether
    b. The number of employees in the workplace
    c. The types of insurance the company offers
    d. The amount of the health premium he is paying

3. Craig is working in an HR position where he wants to find the best possible employees for certain tasks. What form of HR work is Craig handling?
    a. Strategic
    b. Senior
    c. Administrative
    d. Directorial

4. Susan is finding possible candidates based on their backgrounds and less on corporate goals. This is what form of HR work?
    a. Administrative
    b. Strategic
    c. Directorial
    d. Operational

5. Sally is the CEO of a business and has a clause in her contract that states she will earn $50 in severance pay and stock options if she loses her job due to an acquisition or takeover. What does Sally have in this situation?
   a. Golden parachute
   b. Golden handshake
   c. Executive perquisites
   d. Investment benefits

6. Alice recently worked 40 hours in a week and had to work for 10 hours during the Thanksgiving holiday. Is she eligible for overtime pay?
   a. Yes
   b. No
   c. She can earn half pay
   d. This is based on the employer's discretion

7. Michael is a senior executive who recently worked 50 hours in one week. Can he earn overtime pay?
   a. Yes
   b. No
   c. He can earn half pay
   d. The CEO of his business must decide

8. Larry is joining a business' board of directors. He is being hired with the belief that he will provide a unique outside perspective to the business. What kind of worker is Larry?
   a. Ethical director
   b. Outside director
   c. Chief Audit Officer
   d. Consultant

9. Randall has reached the highest possible amount that he can contribute to his 401(k) plan. What can Randall use next to have more money for his retirement plan?
   a. Point of Service plan
   b. Excess deferral plan
   c. Cash balance plan
   d. Money-purchase plan

10. George has proposed a change to the business statement or terms of operation for the company. Management is reviewing George's idea and is debating and amending his proposal. Part of this includes rewriting some of the details. What is this action known as?
   a. Lobbying
   b. Holding
   c. Discharging
   d. Marking

11. A company that has been in the clothing retail industry for a while wants to move into other industries and is going to leave the clothing sector. What is the company doing in this situation?
   a. Reengineering
   b. Restructuring
   c. Divestiture
   d. Refinancing

12. Brian has to attend physical therapy every month for disability. However, his employer states he cannot be absent more than five times in a six-month period. After the sixth therapy session during the sixth month, he is fired. He will then file a lawsuit under the ADA. A court may declare that the business was discriminatory against Brian. What should be done to rectify the situation?
   a. The work position he had should be removed
   b. He should be rehired and have his schedule organized based on his physical needs
   c. Pay for Brian's therapy sessions
   d. Allow for new terms in the attendance policy

13. Louis lost his job, but it was not through his own fault. Can he earn unemployment benefits in this situation?
    a. He can get all his benefits
    b. The business can decide on this
    c. No benefits are available
    d. Louis would have to meet new standards to get those benefits

14. Beth has a physical ability and can still do her job, but she lost her job anyway. Can she apply for unemployment benefits?
    a. She has to prove she is disabled in some way
    b. She has to prove she had the best possible conduct
    c. There needs to be a review of why she lost her job
    d. The relevance of the job should be considered

15. Clyde is hiring Claudia to work at his business because he just has an intuitive feeling that she's the right person for the job. Clyde is hiring her based on his:
    a. First impression
    b. Gut feeling
    c. Sudden demand
    d. Stereotype

16. Craig, a white person, chooses to hire Annie, an Asian person, to work in his accounting firm. Craig did not consider other people from different backgrounds for the job. Why would Craig have done this?
    a. First impression
    b. Stereotype
    c. Sudden demand
    d. Contrast

17. Dana is a worker who earns about $40,000 a year and is only eligible for work in the creative department in the workplace. What is Dana interpreted as being?
    a. Exempt
    b. Non-exempt
    c. Individual creative
    d. Executive creative

18. Helga prefers to operate her business group based on how mature the people in the group are. She uses the maturity level of people to decide what ideas they might work with most often. What theory of leadership is Helga following?
    a. Path-Goal theory
    b. Hersey-Blanchard theory
    c. Gantt grid
    d. Blake-Mouton grid

19. John got a 90% score on his first employment test. He got a 40% score on the second test that he completed. What concern should be reviewed in this situation?
    a. Correlation
    b. Reliability
    c. Concurrent validity
    d. Predictive validity

20. Tim has money in an IRA, but he plans on making an early withdrawal from the account. What will happen?
    a. The money he withdraws will be taxed
    b. He will experience a 10% penalty
    c. He will receive a 15% penalty
    d. He will be penalized based on whether he is over or under 59.5 years of age

21. Cheryl heard that her boss is going to be leaving soon, thus prompting her to speak with an HR manager about a possible new opening. What is Cheryl doing?
    a. Bidding
    b. Posting
    c. Specification
    d. Furlough

22. Amelia is motivated to work based on her personal satisfaction and is not as concerned about pay as other people might be. What does this mean Amelia has?
    a. Intrinsic reward
    b. Personal fulfillment
    c. Personal ambition
    d. Individual productivity

23. After interviewing ten different candidates, Thomas has given all the candidates nearly the same rating. What form of interview bias is Thomas expressing?
    a. Stereotypes
    b. Leniency
    c. Noise
    d. Tendency

24. Chris was not given attention during his interview process. This is due to his low score on an employment test. The person interviewing Chris is experiencing what type of bias?
    a. Contrast
    b. Horn
    c. Competency
    d. Predictive

25. Ryan is planning a medical exam for many of the people at his business. When would he be able to get that exam ready for people to complete?
    a. When the exam is going to support the workplace
    b. When all people in a job category can work with the exams
    c. When all the exams are job-related
    d. When the business demands new reviews

26. Lewis has experienced permanent disability. Will he be able to withdraw from his 401(k) fund early?
    a. Yes
    b. No
    c. Depends on his disability
    d. Relative to his work situation

27. A workplace has to establish new accessibility standards for disabled workers. These may be interpreted as undue hardships provided that:
    a. The cost is high
    b. The finances of the business will be impacted
    c. It would be difficult for management to get this ready due to the immense number of items needed
    d. The burden on the employer is significant

28. Sandra was part of a discrimination proceeding where her employer was fined. Sandra was then fired a few weeks later. Under what category can Sandra file a charge?
    a. Harassment
    b. Quid pro protection
    c. Discrimination
    d. Retaliation

29. Tony is receiving about a dollar extra per hour because he is working on the third shift at his place of employment. This extra pay is called:
    a. Differential pay
    b. Hazard pay
    c. Premium pay
    d. Equity pay

30. A business is going to use a safe-harbor provision to resolve the payroll errors that were found. What does this practice include?
    a. Good faith commitments are not needed
    b. Certain actions may dictate what goes about
    c. Employees may be reimbursed for inappropriate deductions
    d. None of the above

31. Janet will go through asynchronous training before she is employed. What would this part of training be called?
    a. Rated training
    b. Computer training
    c. Self-paced training
    d. Control timing

32. Anthony is working as a cashier at a supermarket. Would he be eligible for vestibule training?
    a. Yes
    b. No
    c. Depending on the role
    d. Based on budget

33. As an HR director, Louis is reviewing staffing needs based on how the training in the workplace and which employees currently require some form of help. What form of forecasting is Louis using in this scenario?
    a. Future map
    b. Scenario analysis
    c. Delphi technique
    d. Lateral thinking

34. Ryan is suing his employer because the employer does not have a health care plan for its employees. Under what type of legislation can Ryan sue the employer?
    a. ERISA
    b. EEOC
    c. COBRA
    d. None of the above

35. Tony is under the age of 39. Can he still be protected by the Age Discrimination in the Employment Act?
    a. Yes
    b. No
    c. Depends on the field he is in
    d. The case would immediately be discarded if he were to file one

36. Claude has worked more than eight hours a day in the last few days at his job in a manufacturing plant. Is he allowed to receive time and a half for his work?
    a. He can get double time instead
    b. Time and a half is allowed
    c. The regular pay only
    d. Depends on the number of hours he worked in the week

37. The Jones Company has two separate divisions - one of those divisions being unionized and the other not being a part of the union. What could this be interpreted as?
    a. Secondary change
    b. Ally division
    c. Alter Ego
    d. Double-breasting

38. The Jones Company and the Davis Organization both operate with the same ownership and use operations that link to one another. They both use the same labor control functions and operate with similar purposes. The two businesses can be interpreted as being which of the following concepts?
    a. Double-breasting
    b. Alter Ego
    c. Ally division
    d. Straight-line operation

39. A company's union is going on strike as a means of getting better work conditions. Is the strike sensible?
    a. It is lawful
    b. It is an unfair labor
    c. It is unlawful
    d. This is illegal according to the NLRB

40. The HR system in the Jones Business needs to be analyzed during an investigation over discriminatory processes in the hiring process. For what purpose can the system be reviewed?
    a. To find trends and ratio reports
    b. To summarize the work in one's field
    c. To get data on affirmative action functions
    d. To see if a group is complying with EEO-1 forms

41. The Fox Agency has issued a series of yellow dog contracts for some of its employees. These contracts state:
    a. Employees cannot join unions by signing agreements
    b. Joining a union can cause someone to be fired
    c. Both a and b
    d. Neither a nor b

42. The Fox Agency is gauging its employees based on a few standards. This includes working with a survey that will be sent out to about half of the customers that the agency has served. What is the agency using when determining who will be questioned?
    a. Distribution
    b. Sample
    c. Prerequisite
    d. General analysis

43. Michael needs to file a ULP with the NLRB after a certain event took place. How much time does he have to file the ULP?
    a. 1 month
    b. 3 months
    c. 6 months
    d. 12 months

44. A new union is being formed at a supermarket to help support the needs of the employees. The union should do all but one the following to be recognized.
    a. Hold an election
    b. Produce an LMRA petition
    c. Ask for recognition
    d. Produce authorization cards

45. The NLRB is considering an election about employee functions. What percentage of eligible employees must support the petition for the election to take place?
    a. 20%
    b. 30%
    c. 50%
    d. 60%

46. Wesley is preparing a neutrality agreement to be signed with a union, although he is uncertain as to what the agreement is about. What does this mean?
    a. He is agreeing to an NLRB election
    b. He will remain neutral to union efforts
    c. He will not try to do anything to oppose a union's actions
    d. He will stay with the union even when it is absorbed by another entity

47. Mary is starting a new budget for her business. In this, all expenses must be justified. Other than that, she is starting from scratch. What is she engaging in?
    a. Zero-based budget
    b. Historic budget
    c. Correlation budget
    d. Formula budget

48. Willis has a relationship with another person in the workplace who is disabled. Willis feels that he is being discriminated against according to the ADA. Does he have a case?
    a. He has a case with the Rehabilitation Act
    b. Yes
    c. No
    d. The manager must be consulted first

49. A CEO at a tech firm has received information about a worker's inability to perform certain functions in the workplace due to medical concerns. What should the CEO do?
    a. Analyze the medical documentation
    b. Remove the employee
    c. Establish the appropriate accommodations
    d. Reach a benefits provider for additional info

50. Carl is a high-level executive in the HR department. He is controlling the resources and assets for a project. He has agreed to fund a major business venture. What role is Carl performing?
    a. Executive
    b. Sponsor
    c. Coordinator
    d. Manager

51. While employed at the industrial plant, Andrey worked for 32 hours from Tuesday to Friday and had Monday off because it was a federal holiday. He then worked for eight hours on Saturday. Is he entitled to overtime pay for that Saturday?
    a. Yes, because he doesn't normally work Saturdays
    b. No, because he did not go beyond 40 hours that week
    c. Yes, because he is working in hazardous conditions
    d. No, because he was already getting some special bonuses

52. There are three people who are actively operating a software production company. One of those people is working in operations while others are not. This type of business can be interpreted as being a:
    a. Strategic partnership
    b. Sole proprietorship
    c. Joint venture
    d. Limited liability entity

53. Greg is going to conduct a salary survey in his HR firm. Which of these surveys isn't going to work for him?
    a. Commissioned
    b. Union
    c. Industry
    d. Government

54. Fareed is going to conduct a performance evaluation in his workplace. What should he not be doing in the situation?
    a. Conduct a 360-degree review
    b. Use the BARS system
    c. Produce a focal review
    d. Rank his employees

55. A business that has 101 to 200 employees in its operation has been found liable for discrimination in hiring. What is the amount the business could be fined for its operations?
    a. $50,000
    b. $75,000
    c. $100,000
    d. $200,000

56. Celia states that there needs to be controlled in the disparity between how much money men and women are earning based on the same functions they do. What is she supporting?
    a. Pay equity
    b. Pay adjustment
    c. Composite equity
    d. Comparable worth

57. Patrick is an independent contractor. Does the 20-factor test work for him?
    a. Yes
    b. No
    c. Only a portion of it
    d. As many details as necessary

58. Samantha states that she has been discriminated against in her workplace because she is pregnant. Can she receive support for her grievance in accordance with Title IX?
    a. Yes
    b. No
    c. It depends on the money she is earning
    d. The grievance cannot be supported

59. Max says that he did not commit perjury on behalf of his employer, but he got fired anyway. What point can Max use in a legal case against his employer?
    a. Contract exception
    b. Duty of good faith
    c. Fraudulent misrepresentation
    d. Public policy exception

60. Susan states that she had her image harmed due to the employer having information and using that data to hurt her reputation. What can Susan use as a basis of a lawsuit?
    a. Undue damage
    b. Harassment
    c. Defamation
    d. Constructive criticism

61. Yolanda is being told that she can have a promotion in her workplace if she sleeps with her manager. What form of sexual harassment is this?
    a. Quid pro quo
    b. Hostile work environment
    c. Tangible action
    d. Unrequited favor

62. Travis is being told to provide employee notice about the FMLA. What is he supposed to do?
    a. Communicate with a person at least 30 days before that person leaves
    b. Reach the employee for a consultation as soon as possible due to an unforeseeable leave
    c. Offer retroactive notification
    d. A and B

63. Harry is actively confirming project details that include managing certain instructions and deciding what should be done to allow a business to progress. He is reviewing differences between job performance and expectations and is reviewing where the issues exist. What is Harry doing in this situation?
    a. Leading
    b. Planning
    c. Controlling
    d. Organizing

64. Zack is going to organize a centralized approach for how his business is to operate. When would it be best for him to do this?
    a. When he needs customer feedback as soon as possible
    b. When he needs to deliver leads sooner
    c. To determine expansion tasks
    d. To utilize labor accordingly

65. Juan is operating his HR group to determine the objectives that his team should follow in the future. This includes looking at goals and tasks based on what works in the environment and how HR goals are to be met. What are Juan and his HR team working with in this case?
    a. Operations
    b. Action planning
    c. Objective analysis
    d. Department goal reviews

Answers to SHRM-CP Situational Exam 1

1. b. The Equal Employment Opportunity Commission states that it is a violation of the Equal Pay Act when there is clearly unequal compensation for male and female workers.

2. c. The COBRA coverage standard does not cover a plan that only offers life insurance or disability benefits. Jeff can get COBRA benefits if he has fewer hours of employment but has not lost his job altogether.

3. a. Strategic HR is considering long-term plans for growth and finding the best overall decisions for the workplace.

4. d. Operational HR is complying with laws and how everyday tasks can be completed based on backgrounds and other qualifying data.

5. a. A golden parachute is compensation that a person will get due to a takeover or acquisition. The money involved might dissuade some parties from trying to take over a group.

6. b. Overtime pay is applicable when someone works more than 40 hours in a week and does not apply to work on a holiday. Individual businesses have the option to add extra pay for holidays, but they are not obligated.

7. a. Because Michael worked more than 40 hours in a week, he is certainly entitled to overtime pay.

8. b. An outside director is a person who is not a stakeholder or employee of the company. The opinions he offers are unbiased and they are well outside of what the business normally does.

9. b. An excess deferral plan does not impose limits as to what one can contribute.

10. d. The marking process includes reviewing the quality of a bill.

11. c. Divestiture is a process where an asset is reduced through liquidation, a sale, or closure among other events. This is the opposite of an investment and is done to consolidate a business or keep it from being too expensive to operate.

12. b. The ADA states that the employee should be rehired with the terms of one's work being adjusted based on his disability. The key is to allow for accommodation when helping a person to manage a disability. In this case, his work hours can be adjusted.

13. a. Unemployment benefits are available when a person is unemployed for reasons that they cannot control. This is different from gross misconduct, which is an event that occurs due to the employee's own actions.

14. b. The worker can get unemployment benefits if she expressed the proper conduct on the job.

15. b. A gut feeling refers to the intuition that one has for hiring a candidate.

16. b. A stereotype occurs when a person makes a decision based on surface characteristics. In this case, the manager is employing the stereotype that a person of Asian descent is good at math.

17. a. The worker is exempt under the FLSA as a creative professional. The person would qualify for benefits if that person was responsible for the invention or establishment of something in a relevant segment of the business and its general operations.

18. b. The Hersey-Blanchard situational leadership theory states that a person's work actions should be based on the leadership of the situation.

19. b. Reliability focuses on producing consistent results. In this case, the test in question might not be all that reliable because the results are too unusual or are bouncing from one segment to another.

20. d. Tim would be penalized 10% of his contributions if he is under 59.5 years of age.

21. a. Job bidding is an action where a person applies for a position from within the business.

22. a. The intrinsic reward is the general satisfaction that one gets out of the work they do.

23. d. The central tendency may also be called the average. This is an interview bias that shows the tendency of a manager to rate all people as being average.

24. d. A predictive bias occurs when a person's background is reviewed based on the predictions that might have been made.

25. c. The ADA has restrictions on when people are asked about their physical abilities. It is acceptable to ask about their physical abilities if the task requires a person to be physically adept in some way.

26. a. A person can withdraw from a 401(k) early without penalty if they experience permanent disability, debts owed to the IRS, or if a person in the military reserve has been called to active duty for at least 180 days.

27. d. A burden is based on the review of the circumstances surrounding the situation. There may be cases when an employer is unable to manage certain expenses without making dramatic changes.

28. d. Retaliation is an event where a person has been accused of engaging in certain activities that are inappropriate.

29. a. Differential pay occurs when a person receives to pay for work that goes beyond the basic requirements of that job. This may not be interpreted as hazard pay, as that considers dangerous situations.

30. c. There has to be a good faith approach to managing the process of getting one's payments handled accordingly.

31. c. Asynchronous training involves a person using timing standards for training. This is not like synchronous training where everyone is subjected to the same form of training at the same time.

32. a. Vestibule training is near-the-job training where a person is placed in a simulated environment. The cashier has the right to go through the training so he will understand what to do.

33. b. The scenario analysis process includes a qualitative analysis of possible HR demands that may occur. Many events will be reviewed to determine

what the possible HR demand will be in the workplace based on what is now working.

34. d. A business is not obligated to offer retirement benefits to anyone. The ERISA standard is used when the business does actually offer these benefits.

35. b. The ADEA does not cover cases of reverse age discrimination.

36. d. Claude's work should be reviewed based on how many hours he is working in a week. He can get overtime pay if he works beyond 40 hours.

37. d. Double-breasting develops when a person is the owner of a unionized business and a non-unionized business.

38. b. An alter ego occurs when two businesses have the same ownership or management.

39. b. A lawful strike is one that ensures that a business can provide some kind of economic gain. In this case, it is believed that a positive economic gain can occur if working conditions are improved.

40. c. The Human Resource Information System can help identify affirmative action details and on how people are analyzed based on what they can or cannot do when getting a business to grow.

41. c. A yellow dog contract states that a person can be fired for joining a union. The Norris-LaGuardia Act states that such a contract is illegal and that people can join unions without being at risk of losing their jobs for doing so.

42. b. A sample is a grouping of people who may be interviewed at a time. This can be a random series of people surrounding a certain situation or activity.

43. c. ULP is an unfair labor practice. The NLRB states that a ULP report must be filed within six months of when that ULP occurred.

44. b. A petition must be made to the NLRB to have a union officially recognized.

45. b. A petition signed by at least 30% of the employees in the workforce should be filed with an NLRB office before an election may occur.

46. c. The neutrality agreement states that an employer must allow a union to organize. The employer should allow the union to operate even if the employer is not appreciative of some of the things the union is doing.

47. a. A zero-based budget involves a new budget being produced every year without making any references to past budgets.

48. b. The ADA states that a person can receive protection if that person is discriminated against because they had a relationship with a disabled person.

49. a. The medical documentation should be scrutinized and compared to the task that a person is being asked to complete in their job.

50. b. A sponsor is someone who will identify project needs and concerns. The sponsor will ensure that all benefits are fully realized and that any outside issues that might develop can be resolved.

51. b. The FLSA states that overtime pay is only given to those who have worked more than 40 hours in a week. This is regardless of the day of the week that a person is working.

52. d. A limited liability group is one where most of the people involved are investors and they are not involved in daily operations. A person will receive appropriate coverage for work done.

53. b. A union survey is not a salary survey.

54. d. The ranking is comparing employees with one another. This includes looking at which people are the best-performing employees in a work area.

55. c. The largest damage one can be subjected to is $100,000 when the company has from 101 to 200 employees.

56. d. The concept of comparable worth is the belief that men and women should be paid the same for work and have the same experience, skill level,

and responsibilities. Comparable worth may be interpreted as a doctrine, although it is not necessarily a law for all businesses to obey.

57. a. The key part of a 20-factor test is to review how well a person can handle certain jobs in the workplace. A person who is controlled by the employer could be interpreted as an official employee of the company and not as a contractor.

58. c. Title IX states that employees will receive the proper support for necessary medical expenses. This includes support for those who are pregnant and need help with medical costs associated with the pregnancy.

59. d. The public policy exception states that an employee is wrongfully discharged when the person being fired violates public policy.

60. c. Defamation occurs when a person's image has been harmed due to some kind of action that involves their personal information or image being used improperly. Defamation often occurs when a person is trying to find a new job and uses an older employer as a reference.

61. a. Quid pro quo harassment occurs when a person tries to offer something to an employee in exchange for sexual favors.

62. d. A person who is dealing with a foreseeable leave should contact management at least 30 days ahead of time. For unforeseeable leave, the employee needs to contact management as soon as possible to resolve the situation.

63. c. Controlling works when a person is confirming the quality of a task and is seeing that the proper organizational resources are used. Any deviations in the regular functionality in the workplace should be explored and discussed if necessary.

64. c. A decentralized decision is the decision-making process involving many groups in one organization.

65. b. Action planning involves producing a tactical plan that looks at actions that are to be sent to particular employees with specific deadlines in mind. Specific goals are to be incorporated in the process.

SHRM-CP Exam 2

1. Is it lawful for an employer to replace an older worker with a younger work as a means of reducing the amount of money on the payroll?
   a. Yes
   b. No
   c. Depends on the industry
   d. Depends on how many people

2. The FLSA requires a business to record all but one of the following:
   a. Hourly pay rate
   b. When one is paid
   c. Pay period covered
   d. All are included

3. What does an employment brand entail?
   a. Recruitment slogan
   b. Serial number
   c. Product name
   d. Perception of working

4. You can review resumes to see if a person meets the necessary requirements for a job. Is this an employment decision?
   a. Yes
   b. No
   c. Further testing is needed
   d. Works better when determining salary

5. What makes it important for you to send a job offer to someone in writing?
   a. To provide employment details
   b. DoL requirement
   c. This is actually a bad idea
   d. State laws in your area

6. What makes an employment interview valuable?
   a. This helps you to measure people based on how well they perform
   b. You will review people based on general regulations
   c. For purview purposes
   d. To see that you gage people based on certain standards

7. What makes a long-term goal valuable in the workplace?
   a. Influence many inside factors
   b. Allow for resources to be organized well
   c. Separate effects of culture versus other needs
   d. Show how people are organized and ready to work

8. The Equal Pay Act prohibits improper wage differentials for:
   a. Age
   b. Sex
   c. Race
   d. Work experience

9. What is not considered to be a pay differential?
   a. Overtime
   b. Hazard pay
   c. Shift pay
   d. Base pay

10. An employee holds a non-forfeitable contribution to a pension plan. What is this known as?
    a. Trust
    b. Qualified plan
    c. Non-qualified plan
    d. Vesting

11. Which of the following is a mandatory deduction on a paycheck?
    a. Wage garnishment
    b. Union dues (for businesses that operate with unions)
    c. 401(k) contributions
    d. Health benefits

12. What is an income statement?
    a. A review of profits and losses
    b. A review of money flowing
    c. An analysis of where the money goes within the business
    d. A look at how much money individuals are earning

13. What are accrued expenses?
    a. Any payments you are making to employees
    b. Accurately reported payments
    c. Expenses that have not been paid yet
    d. Income that is yet to be earned

14. What type of chart should be used to analyze attendance impacts in your workplace and how they influence what happens in the workplace?
    a. Recognition diagram
    b. Scatter plot
    c. Gantt chart
    d. None of the above

15. What is the first thing that has to be done when attempting to get people in the workplace to adapt to changes?
    a. Introduce the change
    b. Review resistance
    c. Talk with employees
    d. Communicate the change

16. What would a manager do to inspire people to be their own leaders?
    a. Laissez-faire leadership
    b. Controlling
    c. Transaction leadership
    d. Transformational leadership

17. How often can a Summary Plan Description or SPD be provided to workers?
    a. Every year
    b. Every three years
    c. Every five years
    d. Every ten years

18. What does the Copyright Act not cover?
    a. Music composition
    b. American government work
    c. Content by children under the age of 18
    d. Duplicated content

19. Which of the following is not one of the parts of the DMAIC process used in Six Sigma?
    a. Control
    b. Measure
    c. Analyze
    d. Invest

20. A business can establish an alternative to recover property and content in the event of an emergency or other concern in the workplace. This plan is called a:
    a. Continuity plan
    b. Emergency response plan
    c. Disaster recovery plan
    d. Backup plan

21. A person who is injured and is able to do some of the duties of their job should be entitled to:
    a. Modified actions
    b. Reasonable accommodation
    c. Proper medical review
    d. New position

22. A recognition strike is:
    a. Getting a business to recognize a trade union
    b. Having a business allow a group to have more economic power
    c. Demanding new tasks for people to work with
    d. Providing honors for people

23. A sit-down strike is:
    a. People staying in a break room
    b. People sitting outside the business and protesting certain things
    c. People not willing to travel for work-related tasks
    d. People taking possession of their work stations

24. What should you be asking yourself when working on a strategic plan?
    a. Where should the business go?
    b. Who is leading the work?
    c. Who are you competing with?
    d. What monies are needed for operation purposes?

25. An employee who has met certain work standards is not required to take a test. This is considered:
    a. Positive reinforcement
    b. Negative reinforcement
    c. Exclusion
    d. Preferential treatment

26. Arbitration is a process for resolving disputes. What makes this form of resolution distinct?
    a. Takes place outside a court
    b. A separate person decides the proper award
    c. The case is legally binding on both sides
    d. All of the above

27. Mediation is another way of resolving disputes. What makes this way unique?
    a. Bidding is used to decide who is right
    b. The situation is ignored for a few weeks
    c. New rules may be imposed based on the dispute in question
    d. A third-party intervenes

28. A group on strike may picket when the main employer's work site is within the site of another employer. What type of picketing is this known as?
    a. Hot cargo
    b. Common situs
    c. Neutral
    d. Consumer

29. A worker might learn about their routines the best through a hands-on approach. This is what type of learner?
    a. Auditory
    b. Blended
    c. Visual
    d. Tactile

30. An HR organizer responsible for operating a team-building practice should do the following to keep an operation successful and effective:
    a. Reward people for the work they are doing
    b. Make participation mandatory
    c. Measure how well a program works
    d. Gather support from management

31. A person may be asked to complete many new tasks in addition to their existing line of work. This is known as:
    a. Enrichment
    b. Expansion
    c. Enlargement
    d. Infusion

32. A program may be established to help people who have lost their jobs and need help finding new ones. What is this program called?
    a. Severance support
    b. Outplacement help
    c. Indirect benefits
    d. WARN support

33. A person who has participated in an international project and is returning to their country of origin to work must be re-integrated. This would require the following practice:
    a. Expatriation
    b. Repatriation
    c. Integration
    d. Geocentralization

34. Which of these is not considered to be a form of quantitative analysis?
    a. Time-series review
    b. Delphi study
    c. Ratio review
    d. Simulation model

35. An employee deposits money to a retirement plan in the workplace. When will that money be vested?
    a. Right away
    b. After a few years
    c. After five years of cliff vesting
    d. Based on graduated vesting rules

36. What can be said about a tort?
    a. It is an illegal act
    b. It can lead to a criminal case
    c. Only hourly workers can do this
    d. A and B

37. Can wrongful termination be interpreted as a tort?
    a. Yes, it is wrong
    b. Yes, all people should be treated the same
    c. No, sometimes there is a reason
    d. No, a contract is not a tort

38. What can be said about a defined benefit plan in the workplace?
    a. Employee contributions are required
    b. The plan points one can use have increased in recent time
    c. Benefits are to be protected
    d. Money can be purchased in some situations

39. A Flexible Spending Account might have some funds that are not used. What will happen to those funds if they are not used?
    a. Funds are brought back to the employee
    b. Anything that one does not spend will be lost
    c. Funds have to roll over to another period
    d. The IRS pays the funds back to the person who contributed them

40. The vision for an HR department includes:
    a. Short-term goals
    b. Long-term goals
    c. Major objectives
    d. A mission statement

41. After determining the stakeholders in the workplace and what those people might be expecting of your business, you can focus on:
    a. Setting expectations
    b. Determining the input you anticipate
    c. Planning your questions
    d. Determining international standards for interacting with others in your work environment

42. Which of the following skills does a transformational leader have?
    a. Power
    b. Emotional intelligence
    c. Ethical understanding
    d. All of the above

43. When you are recognizing people based on the particular contributions they are providing to your workplace, you are showing:
    a. Kindness
    b. Integrity
    c. Justice
    d. Transcendence

44. Transcendence is a part of managing values that includes:
    a. Valuing specific shareholders
    b. Focusing on a very specific task
    c. Going beyond the rules for helping people
    d. Putting stakeholders first

45. The best way to manage a challenging situation in the workplace is to:
    a. Analyze the issue with others
    b. Figure out the monetary aspects of the work
    c. Put personal motivations to one side
    d. Analyze unique ideas for help

46. Employee communication should be open to all people. What would it mean when you are allowing your workers to interact with the people who are responsible for running the business?
    a. Bottom-up communication
    b. Top-down communication
    c. Interactivity
    d. Control for the work environment

47. The central philosophy of your business should be easy to handle:
    a. A specific situation
    b. Certain people who can help you out
    c. Working on many tasks at a time
    d. Very few words

48. The communicator gives a message to the intended receiver. What does the communicator expect?
    a. Response
    b. Feedback
    c. Analysis
    d. Control

49. What can be said about using social media to communicate with your audience?
    a. You can reach a large number of people
    b. You may not reach the people you want to reach
    c. The content can be highly detailed
    d. A and B

50. An oral presentation is best for conveying an HR strategy when:
    a. You need to have immediate feedback
    b. You have lots of details to hammer out
    c. You want to reach a specific audience
    d. You have little time for getting something ready

51. A written report will be ideal for your HR strategy plans when:
    a. You have a large audience to work with
    b. You need immediate feedback
    c. You have a massive amount of details to review
    d. You want to get something out as soon as possible

52. A small group is better for discussing plans instead of a larger group if:
    a. You have too much content to handle at a time
    b. You need to talk about sensitive data
    c. You are trying to simplify things of value
    d. You want to get a message out regardless of its overall context

53. An H-2A visa may be provided to:
    a. An agricultural worker
    b. A non-agricultural worker
    c. A person in a specialty organization
    d. None of the above

54. You can hire a person for an H-2A or H-2B visa if that person is:
    a. From an eligible country
    b. Has proper experience
    c. Plans on working for up to one year or three years with renewal
    d. All of the above

55. A person who has an H-1B visa may be able to become a permanent resident of the United States. This is provided that the person has:
    a. A clean record
    b. Been sponsored by an employer
    c. Has paid the proper taxes
    d. Information about the laws regarding working in the United States

56. The main question to ask employees about how they feel about the leaders in the workplace is to find out:
    a. If those people believe in and trust the leaders that they are working with
    b. If those people feel they are being compensated well enough
    c. If they can work without barriers
    d. If they can work on their own authority

57. The work-life balance in the workplace can be attained through:
    a. On-site childcare
    b. Gym memberships
    c. Concierge services
    d. All of the above

58. The preparation process of getting a negotiation moving forward may include:
    a. Determining payments
    b. Analyzing the work
    c. Making concessions
    d. Reviewing contact information

59. Due diligence is:
    a. Planning work on time
    b. Completing tasks within budget
    c. Reviewing the details in a matter
    d. Analyzing the work being planned

60. What can be done to resolve cognitive problems in the workplace?
    a. Offer strong leadership
    b. Review conflict resolution processes
    c. Perform on-the-job training
    d. Conduct regular analytics to determine what is contributing to problems

61. An agile business is able to:
    a. Prioritize strategic decisions
    b. Increase profits
    c. Reviewing employee schedules
    d. A and C

62. A merger or acquisition will require:
    a. A cultural assessment
    b. Changes in the laws in the workplace
    c. A revision of the mission statement
    d. A review of the employees in the workplace

63. The Delphi technique used to review ideas for the workplace must:
    a. Take place in remote locations
    b. Be a freewheeling approach to finding ideas
    c. Acknowledge unique faults or ideas
    d. Include contact with legal groups for details on the situation

64. A nominal group technique is the production of a comprehensive list of ideas or alternatives. The main purpose of the technique is that it is:
    a. Detailed
    b. Remote
    c. Structured
    d. Legally binding

65. A stratification chart is also called a:
    a. Flow chart
    b. Histogram
    c. Control chart
    d. Pareto chart

66. What can a check sheet review?
    a. Occurrences of certain events
    b. Times when things happened
    c. The types of events that are taking place
    d. All of the above

67. What type of culture relates to activities that focus on loyalty?
    a. Market
    b. Clan
    c. Adhocracy
    d. Hierarchy

68. What culture focuses more on taking risks?
    a. Market
    b. Clan
    c. Adhocracy
    d. Hierarchy

69. The main consideration for downsizing when managing a business is cutting down the work due to:
    a. A lack of funds
    b. Expenses being too high
    c. No need for certain assets
    d. Managing legal considerations

70. A company that offers many brands of foods may be considered:
    a. An extended organization
    b. An authority group
    c. A divestiture
    d. A monopolistic organization

71. A turnover analysis reviews details on how people might be leaving the workplace due to disability, resignations, disciplinary actions, and other common concerns. The goal of the analysis is to:
    a. Determine why people are leaving the workforce
    b. Identify the departments that have people leaving
    c. See how the business groups change due to different factors
    d. Note how supplies in the workplace might change in value and arrangement

72. A project employee would be hired to:
    a. Train people to follow new skills and habits
    b. Complete specific tasks
    c. Do seasonal work
    d. Open new locations

73. Payrolling is a practice to:
    a. Establish unique rules for what people may do for work in a situation
    b. Forward that person through a temp agency
    c. Reach people for contracts that have fewer work duties
    d. Analyze the number of people who might want to work for you

74. You can use a mortgage subsidiary for an employee who is relocating if:
    a. They want to buy a property of a certain value
    b. There's a need to encourage a person to choose a specific property
    c. The mortgage rates are starting to rise
    d. An employee is willing to accept a specific change in position to another location

75. One way to encourage a worker to take in a position that requires relocation is to:
    a. Purchase the person's home in the old city so they can buy elsewhere
    b. Analyze the taxation rules in the workplace
    c. Find new schools for their kids
    d. Find new jobs for other members of the family in the new city

76. After finding a candidate in the succession planning process, you need to:
    a. Determine the wage they expect
    b. Decide if you need more internal or external candidates
    c. Maintain a skills inventory
    d. Establish group rules for promotions

77. Termination provisions can include all the following except:
    a. Buyout information
    b. Causes for why someone could possibly be terminated
    c. Golden parachute information (for executive positions)
    d. Advance notice

78. What is an example of an internal dimension of a person?
    a. Work style
    b. Friendships
    c. Skin color
    d. Values

79. Organizational dimensions can relate to:
    a. Preferential treatment of others
    b. Assumptions based on gender
    c. Standards for making decisions on careers
    d. Determining who people are going to contact when completing certain tasks

80. What makes diversity helpful for the workplace?
    a. It makes your candidate pool larger
    b. It makes people more creative
    c. People will be less likely to develop conflicts
    d. Customers may be more attracted to your business

81. What allows a person to be eligible for USERRA benefits?
    a. Disability
    b. Seasonal employment
    c. Working in other positions at the same time
    d. All of the above

82. What type of financial benefit will not require a person to contribute as a vested interest?
    a. Cash balance plan
    b. 401(k)
    c. Money-purchase plan
    d. FSA

83. What makes an incentive stock option ideal for a worker?
    a. It is not taxed at exercise
    b. It is unlimited in value
    c. The value is related to market prices of the shares at a grant date
    d. A and C

84. A non-qualified stock option will be taxed as:
    a. Capital gains on the sale
    b. Regular funds at the time of sale
    c. Money based on income
    d. A review of the value of the stock

85. All of the following are involuntary benefits except:
    a. Life insurance
    b. Medicare
    c. FMLA leave
    d. COBRA benefits

86. A sympathy strike will occur when one union is striking:
    a. Out of concerns for bereavement benefits
    b. To honor a person who experienced a loss in the family
    c. To support another entity in a dispute
    d. To allow for an industry to evolve

87. Work to reduce the time of a process could be interpreted as:
    a. Efficiency drive
    b. Unfreezing
    c. Restructuring
    d. Reengineering

88. People who are part of a group in the workplace and have a common set of interests to manage skills and work may be called a:
    a. Skill transfer team
    b. Knowledge management group
    c. Practice community
    d. Administration community

89. An effort to streamline a managerial effort into a few market segments to allow for better decisions to be made can be interpreted as:
   a. Restructuring
   b. Reengineering
   c. Reorganization
   d. Spinning off segments

90. The collaboration process with stakeholders should require you to:
   a. Know about the stakeholders in question
   b. Plan questions based on what the stakeholders might require
   c. Note the efforts that come with running a business
   d. Identify basic routines in the workplace

91. With regard to managing ethics, a transformational leader will consider:
   a. A sense of grounding
   b. Freedom
   c. Varying ideas
   d. Allowing people to be free to use their own ethical standards for work

92. A transformational leader focuses on long-term results based on:
   a. Producing better profits
   b. Developing the workforce
   c. Identifying possible trends
   d. Noting how different businesses might operate in a market

93. The process for managing strategic change should involve:
   a. Communication
   b. Collaboration
   c. Commitment
   d. All of the above

94. The consideration of justice for a worker will include:
    a. Mutually agreed upon terms for work
    b. Planning specific activities in the workplace
    c. Knowing where the workers are
    d. Planning fair payment plans

95. Is the concept of "do as I say and not as I do" good enough for the workplace?
    a. Always
    b. Never
    c. Depends on the situation
    d. Review your role in the business first

Answers to SHRM-CP Exam 2

1. The Fair Labor Standards Act states that an employer should not replace an over-aged worker with a younger one. This is in spite of how younger people under the age of 20 can be paid less.

2. d. Each of these points may be covered in FLSA standard alongside the total wages paid in a period or when a work week starts.

3. d. The perception of working at a place has to be positive for people to want to work there.

4. b. You will need to look at various standards surrounding how well people might work and what needs to be done when reviewing them.

5. a. You can use these employment details to let your workers understand what is happening in the workplace.

6. b. The review process should be based on various guidelines based on how you will hire those people.

7. b. You can use long-term goals to decide on some of the long-term activities that will take place.

8. b. Men and women are expected to be paid the same amount of money for the same type of job. The content of the job is the main factor to determine pay.

9. d. The base pay is a part of the general compensation that an employer will provide. The other three options are differential pay standards.

10. d. Vesting occurs when an employee is given rights over stock incentives or other bonuses that cannot be forfeited.

11. a. A wage garnishment is a standard deduction set by the court that is imposed to satisfy a debt.

12. a. The income statement shows profits and losses based on revenues and expenses during a work period. The revenues can be analyzed to see if there is a net profit being realized.

13. c. An accrued expense is something that has been logged but not yet paid. You will have to pay that expense at a later date.

14. b. A scatter plot shows how there is a relationship between two variables. You can use this to identify a link between attendance and how certain people work on particular tasks.

15. b. If you experience resistance, you must explain to the workers who are resistant to why the change is recommended and how it will be beneficial to them.

16. d. A transformational leader will inspire people to do the right thing. This does not necessarily have as much freedom as what a laissez-faire leader offers, but the support is still considerable.

17. c. The ERISA law states that an SPD must be provided every five years. This includes information on all the changes that have occurred in the workplace and how they might have impacted the workers.

18. b. American government work cannot be copyrighted in any form.

19. d. The Six Sigma process focuses on the steps of Design, Measure, Analyze, Improve, and Control.

20. c. A disaster recovery plan will detail what a business should do to recover and restore its information and content if an emergency ever takes place for any reason.

21. a. Modified actions, or modified duty, involve a temporary work assignment for a person who is recovering from a medical issue. The

person can resume modified work if that person has been cleared by a medical professional.

22. a. A recognition strike requires a business to accept terms demanded by a union. This is essentially a practice to get the business to start accepting the demands of the union.

23. d. A sit-down strike is where people go to their workplaces and sit and do nothing until their demands are met. This is an illegal action.

24. a. Your planning should focus on where you are, where you will go, how you'll get somewhere, and when you will get there.

25. b. Negative reinforcement encourages people to behave positively by taking away perks or benefits.

26. d. Arbitration helps to ensure that a dispute can be resolved outside of a court. However, a court has the right to enforce the results of the arbitration hearing.

27. d. The mediator in a mediation action should be someone who recognizes the needs of both sides of a dispute. This includes ensuring that the parties in the dispute can have their concerns heard in a proper forum.

28. b. A common situs picketing action is illegal, which involves unfair treatment of others who share a workplace and are not a part of the strike.

29. d. A tactile learner can also be called a kinesthetic learner. The person does well when they directly participate in the learning process.

30. d. Management can support a task to ensure that employees can complete the work in question. Employees may not be motivated if they interpreted certain actions to be unnecessary or not all that important.

31. c. Enlargement is a process where the duties in one's line of work have been increased. This is different from expansion in that expansion would involve fields of work changing.

32. b. Outplacement is an employee being sent to a new job in a different market. The goal is to help an employee get used to the new field of work.

33. b. Repatriation is where someone has been out in a field of work for a while and is resuming his duties.

34. b. The Delphi study involves communicating with people and determining the general opinions of many people in the workplace.

35. a. The vesting process means that someone has the right to handle their own funds right away. That person has full control over the funds and has the option to use them as one desires.

36. d. A tort is an event involving illegal activities that may be reviewed in a criminal court. A tort could be conducted by any person in the workplace and should be treated with caution.

37. d. The tort is supposed to be a wrongful action that can lead to some form of liability. A contract should not be interpreted as a type of tort.

38. c. Protection is a particular benefit being given at retirement. The content that is to be protected will vary based on the situation, so the employee will have to review the terms of the benefits they might receive.

39. b. An FSA allows a person to roll over $500 in unused funds into the account for the next year, but that would be the limit. The employer has the right to use the unused funds.

40. b. Your vision is a plan for what you want to do in the future and how you will use data.

41. a. The expectations you have must be relevant to the work.

42. d. A transformational leader will focus on providing new perspectives to a situation and to help people recognize great ideas for how they can work.

43. a. Kindness is a value that may express positivity and care for many people within the work environment.

44. d. A stakeholder is a person who relies on the success of the business.

45. c. Personal motivations and values may interfere and unfairly influence your choices and affect your decisions and reflect your biases.

46. a. Bottom-up communication means that the people on the lower end of employee hierarchy are given the opportunity to interact with superiors and management and express their concerns.

47. d. Your philosophy should be stated briefly, preferably fewer than ten words.

48. b. Feedback is a response that a person might provide to another person, not necessarily their superior. However, it often is in answer to something management has proposed.

49. d. Social media can help you reach a wide audience.

50. a. An oral presentation can be given to as many or as few people as you wish. The presentation is used to share details with an audience of any size.

51. c. A written report gives an overview of the status of the business including staffing, work production, revenues, and expenses.

52. b. There is a possibility that the information might be highly sensitive and should be released to only a few people and not the entire employee population.

53. a. An agricultural worker would be eligible for an H-2A visa.

54. d. An H-2A or H-2B visa work can be from a country that has received the approval of the Secretary of State or the Secretary of Homeland Security. The person must have experience in the field in which they are intending to work. A person can also be allowed to work for a year and can be extended to three years with the proper application being filed.

55. b. Sponsorship provides assurance so that the worker can apply for permanent residence.

56. a. The leaders in the work environment need to be people who agree to work with others at a time.

57. d. A sense of work-life balance can include many benefits. Part of this includes looking at possible initiatives for taking care of children, managing appointments, and support for a worker's health needs.

58. c. Concessions are typically a means of ensuring that the negotiation process can go forward in a positive way.

59. c. Due diligence ensures that the information is adequate and accurate to resolve certain concerns.

60. c. Cognitive problems may be issues where a person is uncertain about what might work in a professional environment.

61. a. Agility is being able to adapt to and handle events that might happen.

62. a. A cultural assessment will review how the culture within the workplace may change.

63. a. The Delphi technique focuses on getting in touch with many people who are independent and anonymous. The outside review is remote and removed from other things in your company.

64. c. A structure must be planned in this case for seeing that the work being planned is thorough and that there's an overall understanding of what to expect.

65. a. You can use such a chart to find details on certain processes within the work environment.

66. d. A check sheet will identify how your tasks are managed.

67. b. The clan culture develops between people who are tight-knit and know each other well. Loyalty is critical.

68. c. The goal of the adhocracy culture is to see that innovations may be planned.

69. c. Downsizing is when a business has an excess number of materials and determines that they are unnecessary. This is a cost-saving measure.

70. a. An extended organization can include many brands that will work together under the same umbrella.

71. a. The main part of the process is to identify why people are leaving the company.

72. b. A project employee is someone hired for a specific task. The task will have been defined beforehand. This may include a definition of what the task involves and how long the work in question is expected to last.

73. b. Payrolling is using people who have registered with a temp agency. The temp agency will take care of the overall process of handling the payroll. This is appropriate if you are planning temporary projects.

74. c. A mortgage subsidiary covers the expenses associated with paying for a property. This may include help for managing inflation relating to the cost of a house.

75. a. Purchasing the worker's old home ensures that the employee will be able to buy another home at the new location.

76. c. A skills inventory lists the specific functions that a person has to follow in order to do the work successfully.

77. d. In some cases, a person might not be given advance notice of being removed from a position.

78. c. Internal dimensions are defined as properties that a person cannot change.

79. a. The organizational dimensions concentrate on specific things that might change how a business operates.

80. b. Creativity may influence how a job is done.

81. a. Uniformed services members can be covered with these benefits even if they become disabled for any reason.

82. d. An FSA is a flexible spending account. This is not something that is going to require any vesting for a person to participate in.

83. a. The lack of taxation at excise is a benefit, but this may still be taxed as capital gains during the sale process. This is based on the profits that one may gain from the transaction.

84. b. The taxation for a non-qualified stock option is considered regular funds at the time of sale.

85. a. Life insurance is not required by law, although you have the option to possibly attain a discounted policy through your employer depending on the terms associated with your work.

86. c. A sympathy strike occurs when the people who are going on strike are doing so out of support for another entity. This is in spite of the entity on

the sympathy strike not having any direct issues with the group that the strike is against.

87. d. Reengineering is a practice where business processes are adjusted or altered as a means of making it easier for business to remain operational.

88. c. A practice community features people who share the same interests in certain activities or events.

89. a. Restructuring is changing at how a business operates and could include management changes, a product produced, and other business practices.

90. a. Collaboration is necessary for people to work together effectively and to be able to resolve problems or concerns in the workplace.

91. a. Transformational activities focus on identifying ways for a business to grow.

92. b. The proper developmental efforts may be noticed based on how well people evolve over time.

93. d. The three points should be done in order from communication to collaboration to establishing a sense of commitment among the people in the workplace.

94. a. Justice works when people agree to certain standards or rules for work.

95. b. This concept may make it harder for people to function as they resolve various conflicting in the process.

SHRM-CP Situational Exam 2

1. Manny is talking with the media about how the working conditions at his workplace are unhealthy and dangerous. Can this be interpreted as a protected concerted event?
   a. Yes
   b. No
   c. He needs many people to come to help
   d. This depends on who he is talking to in the media

2. Travis says in public that only fools are going to buy the products that his company is making. Can this be interpreted as a protected concerted action?
   a. Yes
   b. No
   c. It depends on where he does this
   d. This varies by industry

3. Tony is looking to recover some of the wages that he lost recently. Which of the following things would he not be able to do?
   a. Get the DOL to support the back wages he lost
   b. Get the DOJ to file a lawsuit so he can get those wages
   c. File a lawsuit on his own
   d. Reach the DOL to file an injunction that would prevent the employer from withholding payments from the past

4. The Jones Company has fewer than 200 employees. The company is going to consolidate and will cause at least 66 of its employees to lose their positions. Does the Jones Company have to provide a WARN notice?
   a. Yes for all employees
   b. Only the managers need the notice
   c. No warning necessary
   d. A public report is best

5. The Davis Industry Group has more than 150 employees. The group is filing for bankruptcy but will receive new capital to allow the business to continue operating, thus preventing a shutdown. Does a WARN notice have to be provided in this case?
    a. Yes for all employees
    b. Only for managers
    c. No warning needed
    d. Depends on the funding source

6. A group is doing business with an entity worth more than $100 million. Executives in the group are going to receive bonuses of $100,000 each for the partnership. What is occurring in this case?
    a. Groupthink
    b. Stereotyping
    c. Fundamental attribution error
    d. Arbitration

7. There are concerns between the Fox Entity and the labor union that represents the employees working for the Fox Entity. A lockout may be established by Fox if which of the following issues takes place?
    a. An employer is directly negotiating with employees
    b. Economic pressure is being imposed on the union
    c. A bargaining impasse is announced
    d. Employees that have been engaging in such disputes can be replaced

8. Tim has been hired to be a facilitator in an independent review of a dispute. He will provide support for the company's stakeholder in this case. What is he going to work as?
    a. Peer reviewer
    b. Arbitrator
    c. Ombudsman
    d. Analyst

9. When looking at how he is going to operate his business, Jason has decided that he needs to provide as little guidance to his workers as possible in the hopes that those people will make their own decisions about how they do their jobs. What is this style of leadership?
    a. Democratic leadership
    b. Laissez-faire rule
    c. A transformative group
    d. Free-thinking approach

10. Sandra wants to be protected as a whistleblower after leaking information about her employer engaging in illegal activities. She has to show a prima facie proof of the violation that took place. What does she need as proof?
    a. Anything that affects her employment
    b. Proof she was in a protected action
    c. Evidence shows she participated in a protected activity that led to a harmful action
    d. All of the above

11. Steve is planning a training program where the employees are expected to ask open-ended questions about their work. This includes having people work together to find solutions and to use reasoning. What type of training is Steve providing his employees?
    a. Simulation
    b. Vestibule
    c. Socratic
    d. None of the above

12. Charles notices that one of his employees has been dealing with alcohol abuse that is keeping him from completing his work. Can Charles use an Employee Assistance Program to help that person?
    a. Yes
    b. No
    c. An outside entity should be contacted first
    d. An intervention needs to be held.

13. Your employer wants you to let the employees know that you are doing certain things at the manager's request. What should you do when reporting to your employer about the situation?

    a. Make a recommendation based on the evidence
    b. Avoid making a recommendation
    c. Ask a vice president for help
    d. Consult a legal group for advice

14. You notice that your company's productivity is declining and that some employees are using certain drugs in the break room. What should you do?
    a. Review the laws surrounding drug use in your state
    b. Confirm that the laws for drug use on the federal level are the same as your state
    c. Contact employees to see what they are doing
    d. Find information on SHRM that declares where drug use is legal

15. Your business is in a state where marijuana is legal. You are going to plan different rules surrounding marijuana use at your place of business. What should you do?
    a. Offer choices to a leadership team
    b. Figure out proper response options
    c. Plan new policies based on what you feel is appropriate
    d. Ask for recommendations from your employees

16. You are aiming to introduce new workplace policies about recreational activities. What should you be doing when talking to the employees?
    a. Let them know about the fun they can have
    b. Explain that all employees should act responsibly in their workplaces
    c. Talk about vacation policies
    d. Explain your attendance rules

17. You have employees who might struggle with certain concerns about medical marijuana use. Are ADA accommodations available for medical marijuana?
    a. This depends on the state
    b. You'll need to ask your managers for help
    c. The federal rule should be considered
    d. No further review is needed

18. You are planning a report based on what a team is doing and how well it is working. Part of this includes reviewing the turnover rate in your workplace. Which type of turnover rate doesn't have to be included in your prepared report?
    a. Current rates
    b. Historic rates within the business
    c. Industry rates
    d. National rates regardless of industry

19. What should your turnover rates be based on?
    a. Department
    b. Business work title
    c. Experience
    d. Anything that makes it easy for you to determine what's working

20. You have information on process activities. What type of analytical point is best to use?
    a. Pareto chart
    b. Six Sigma
    c. Matrix
    d. Pie chart

21. You want to measure details about how many people are working in specific segments of your workplace. What would be used to help you determine the details on who is working where?
    a. Pie chart
    b. Pareto chart
    c. Matrix
    d. Gantt chart

22. Your senior management group will have to analyze your data about what is happening in the workplace. How should the senior management use your data?
    a. Review whether the work in question is good or bad
    b. Produce conclusions
    c. Appreciate your work
    d. Make recommendations

23. Rod is in charge of HR for a business and is looking for employees to help with a volunteer effort in the local community. What can Rod do when finding employees who are willing to participate?
    a. Ask managerial employees to do this
    b. Have people sign up knowing they will not be paid but will represent the company
    c. Pay only the people who transport employees to the event
    d. Allow for overtime pay for everyone who participates

24. You are analyzing a possible employee's personnel file. What might be found in the file that should not be included in your judgment of the employee?
    a. Description of the job
    b. Consent forms
    c. Performance analysis data
    d. Opinions you cannot back up

25. You are trying to produce a five-year budget for your employer based on HR actions. You need to review the organizational plan with the following emphasis:
    a. To create a budget
    b. To determine goals
    c. To look at how you're going to train people versus marketing
    d. To look at what HR activities are the most important

26. You are being tasked to downgrade some of the job titles at your workplace. Is this going to be a violation of compensation laws in the United States?
    a. Depends on the severity of the case
    b. It is always a violation
    c. There's no violation involved
    d. It depends on how many people's job you're considering

27. Alicia is looking for a new supplier to provide refreshments for her company's break room. She has many local companies to choose from, with one of them being owned by her husband. What should she do?
    a. Get her husband to offer a good deal
    b. Avoid working with her husband
    c. Treat her spouse's work with care
    d. Look for outside groups

28. While working at your business, you might come across a concern where a governmental entity is looking to pay for the services you need in exchange for certain favors. Is this an ethical concern?
    a. Yes, it is bribery
    b. Yes, it entails not moving information through correct avenues
    c. No, this is safe
    d. No, the process of exchange is legal

29. There is a sexual harassment investigation at your workplace. There are no witnesses to the issue. However, many co-workers say that the accuser is credible. What should be done?
    a. Let the executive stay in his/her position
    b. Apply the proper discipline based on the situation
    c. Suspend the executive immediately
    d. Allow for further analysis

30. Ryan is working with four women in the same HR office. He is not familiar with how to work with women in such an environment. What is the best thing for Ryan to do?
    a. Don't change anything
    b. Ask the women for feedback
    c. Try to avoid too much interaction
    d. Be pro-active

31. A new work requirement is going to directly influence how your business handles its employees. This will lead to changes in how your HR team operates. You decide to let the legal team of your company handle the situation. Is this a sensible plan?
    a. Yes, as no further hiring is needed
    b. Yes, as this is not your concern
    c. No, as HR professionals are responsible for reviewing such changes
    d. No, as an outside attorney should be contacted instead

32. A manager at a business has a secondary business for office equipment maintenance services. He states that he can get that maintenance team to serve the other business he is working with to provide services at a discount. Is this a suitable action?
    a. Review the possible conflict of interest
    b. Discuss the considerations involved with senior managers
    c. Ask for help surrounding the business and its finances
    d. Determine what is making the work run smoothly

33. One of your HR leaders has been adding metrics to various analytical points in the workplace recently. What limits might there be?
    a. It may be difficult to complete work due to the added metrics involved
    b. There are no limits to worry about
    c. The excess analysis can be a threat
    d. The new metrics should be relevant to what you wish to review or test

34. You have hired a new analyst to review changes in benefit programs. What should your new analyst do first?
    a. Allow managers to hear about what is happening
    b. Review the possible benefits available
    c. Provide literature from benefit providers
    d. Have a registration clerk come in to help you

35. You have been directing HR actions for a few years, and now you are being asked to review your employee data. What is the best thing for you to do in this situation?
    a. Have someone else take care of the project
    b. Have a new computer program help you to analyze what works here
    c. Review the data on your own to find out what results are best
    d. Use an off-site consultant

36. You are attempting to analyze HR functions, but a new federal law has been passed about overtime hours and how employees are to be reimbursed for these hours, and what can be considered as overtime. What impacts should you be aware of?
    a. Anything an outside group recommends
    b. Any legal concerns involved
    c. The new rules as it relates to your business
    d. Having legal help as necessary

37. You are aiming to establish a new relationship with business clients. What is the best thing to do get your relationship off the ground?
    a. Introduce organizational goals
    b. Be complimentary to your employees
    c. List details on procedures
    d. All of the above

38. A company is not offering help to accommodate the family or personal life needs that people in the workplace have. The company is bearing with the added risk of what problem?
    a. Reduced productivity
    b. More people being absent
    c. Expenses for recruiting
    d. All of the above

39. Your HR department is working with ERISA standards to ensure that the company is compliant. How does this affect the risk?
    a. Resolution
    b. Intervention
    c. Mitigation
    d. Avoidance

40. You have had communications with a union that will let you hire non-union workers. However, the union wants the non-union workers to pay a fee for collective bargaining. What is this practice called?
    a. Agency shop
    b. Closed shop
    c. Collective shop
    d. Union shop

41. Your former employer says that he was fired because he didn't commit perjury at your request. The employer has a legal case against you. Why is this?
    a. Public policy exception
    b. Fraudulent misrepresentation
    c. Duty of good faith
    d. Contract exception

42. Tom has been released from his job. He wants unemployment compensation while he is actively looking for a new job. For how long is he allowed to get that compensation that he needs?
    a. 18 weeks
    b. 22 weeks
    c. 26 weeks
    d. 30 weeks

43. You are trying to reduce the state unemployment insurance charges in your workplace. What should you do?
    a. Terminate employees for just cause while having the proper documentation
    b. Review how your management processes are working
    c. Challenge any unemployment claims
    d. All of the above

44. You want to manage your ERISA reports, and you need to keep everything organized. Which of the following is not necessary for you to handle?
    a. Annual report
    b. Summary description
    c. Health report
    d. Participation benefits report

45. You want to plan a diversity and inclusiveness project. What would be the best thing for you to do with this in mind?
    a. Ensure all people have a voice
    b. Use the proper quotas
    c. Analyze people by demographic

d. All for an equal number of people in all segments

46. Your D&I program is being planned based on who will be included and how you're going to make your business similar to others in your field. What should you do in this situation?
   a. Use competitive intelligence
   b. Analyze the quality of your business efforts
   c. Figure out how much money you have for employing people
   d. Analyze various demographics in your area

47. You are tasked with planning a mission statement. What should be your concern?
   a. What is our goal?
   b. What is our purpose?
   c. What will our future be?
   d. A and B

48. You want to reach an OECD member to do business. Where would the right team for your contact be found?
   a. Europe
   b. Africa
   c. Southeast Asia
   d. Russia

49. You are reviewing a situation surrounding a person's involuntary separation from your workplace. What could be said about that person's separation?
   a. The person may have abandoned the job
   b. The person might have died
   c. The person is moving to another office
   d. The person wants to follow a different career

50. A supervisor tells an employee not to worry about their performance rating. However, that employee is fired for poor performance a few weeks later. What can the supervisor be accused of?
    a. Offered an oral contract
    b. Provided improper information
    c. Acted casually
    d. All of the above

51. You want to remove a person from the workplace because of certain actions. What has to be considered?
    a. There must be a valid reason to remove someone from their job
    b. You need to look at the issues involved with the case
    c. You should review the money you are spending
    d. All of the above

52. You are talking with Mary, a person at another business who is offering neutral and informal advice to the stakeholders at her business. Who are you talking to in this case?
    a. Peer reviewer
    b. Arbitrator
    c. Conciliator
    d. Ombudsman

53. A chain operator is going to contract the management out to three market segments to decrease the corporate structure environment. What is this process called?
    a. Restructuring
    b. Reengineering
    c. Contraction
    d. Regression

54. The salary deferrals in your workplace are smaller in size for non-high compensated employees than for those who have more money. You might be looking at different terms based on how these deferrals are working. What test should you conduct at this point?
    a. Disparate deferral
    b. IRS
    c. Excess deferral percentage
    d. Actual deferral percentage

55. You have an employee who has a retirement plan that can cover a specific payout at retirement. What plan is this?
    a. Benefit
    b. Contribution
    c. HMO
    d. Investment

56. You have another employee who has a retirement plan that has no specific benefit, but it allows that employee to make contributions on their own. What kind of a plan is this?
    a. Benefit
    b. Contribution
    c. HMO
    d. Investment

57. You are trying to decrease lateness at your place of business. What type of diagram should be used when you're trying to illustrate what is causing people to be late so that it might influence the productivity in the workplace?
    a. Scatter diagram
    b. Recognition plot
    c. Gantt chart
    d. None of the above

58. You have a piece of work to which you own the copyright starting in 2010 following the death of the person who originally held the copyright. The Copyright Act of 1976 states that you'll have the work protected until:
    a. 2105
    b. 2080
    c. 2100
    d. 2060

59. Your work for hire has copyright starting in 2010 which could be protected from the date of creation to:
    a. 2130
    b. 2140
    c. 2110
    d. 2080

60. You are planning a meeting where the workers will face the front of your room and have them all take notes throughout the work process. What seating layout do you need to use?
    a. Theater
    b. Classroom
    c. Conference
    d. U-shape

61. You are planning an affirmative action review that features a look at the job titles in your workplace and determining the race and gender of people in each department. What analysis are you working with in this case?
    a. Utilization
    b. Job group
    c. Availability
    d. Workforce

62. You want to implement a major change initiative. What should you do as the first step?
    a. Engage with your employees
    b. Determine resistance
    c. Communicate the changes
    d. Reinforce the changes

63. You have a manager in your workplace that is inspiring people to develop leadership and encouraging employee engagement. What type of leadership style is the manager using?
    a. Democratic
    b. Transitional
    c. Transformational
    d. Laissez-faire

64. Some of your employees have received training and you want to analyze their perceptions of the training. What is this analysis called?
    a. Reaction
    b. Learning
    c. Behavior
    d. Analysis

65. You are analyzing your employees on how well they are carrying out particular tasks. You notice certain behaviors. You would use a rating scale to analyze the types of behaviors of those people. What should be used?
    a. Critical incident scale
    b. Full evaluation
    c. Paired comparison
    d. BARS review

Answers to SHRM-CP Situational Exam 2

1. b. A protected concerted event is one where a person is engaging in actions that provide the general protection of employees. In this example, Manny is talking about things that can influence operational functions and employee treatment. Therefore, this is not a protected concerted event.

2. a. Since Travis is not talking about specific people in this situation, this can be interpreted as a protected concerted event.

3. b. Tony can contact the Department of Justice to sue for damages. The DOJ is not going to recover those wages, but it will encourage the business to pay the money owed.

4. a. The WARN Act encourages a notice to be sent out in cases where a business is going to shrink. However, the act does not require notices for events like strikes, failings within the company, or any unplanned issues impacting how the business operates. A 60-day notice should still be provided beforehand.

5. c. No notices have to be given in this situation, as it does not necessarily mean that someone could lose their job due to the issue.

6. c. A fundamental attribution error develops when only personal factors are considered. The situational issues that led to a problem are not being considered.

7. b. Economic pressure is the main goal of a lockout. The company establishes the lockout to keep people from engaging in work. This leads to the employees being encouraged to meet the demands of the owners.

8. c. An ombudsman is a person who is neutral in a dispute. That person will provide independent support to the people in the workplace as a means of resolving a dispute or other issue in the workplace without having a conflict of interest.

9. b. Laissez-faire rule states that a business will allow the workers to make their own decisions. No democratic vote is needed.

10. d. Prima facie proof means that the evidence before a trial is sufficient to prove a case. There should be no evidence to prove what happened.

11. c. Socratic learning involves people asking questions.

12. a. An EAP provides short-term counseling for those with personal problems that might impact how a person is going to handle certain functions in the work environment.

13. a. You will need to make recommendations based on evidence.

14. d. The best solution is to review how you deal with people who are under the influence of certain drugs. This especially is the case if your state has deemed marijuana use legal.

15. d. It helps to gather multiple ideas from people in the workplace.

16. b. All employees in your workplace need to be safe and supportive of one another.

17. a. You would have to review the rules in your state regarding certain activities. Any federal laws that might influence the entire country should also be considered.

18. d. The national rates aren't going to be relevant unless they stipulate the national rates within your specific industry.

19. d. You can work with anything so long as it involves the departments or other groups that you're working with.

20. b. A Six Sigma effort is needed to identify how well your business is operating and if there is an excess amount of waste. The key is to review the quality of the work and what can be done to reduce errors.

21. a. A pie chart is useful when you want to determine which segments in your workplace are the most productive.

22. d. The recommendations will help you identify the concerns that need to be resolved.

23. b. Volunteer work must be unpaid.

24. d. You must avoid relying on opinions or judgments made by reading the files of other people who are interested in working for you.

25. d. Strategic planning is identifying HR functions and how well your business might function.

26. c. There does not appear to be any violations involved in this scenario, although it is best to try to keep the titles the same for convenience purposes. The functions involved will remain the same, thus ensuring there are no issues.

27. b. It is best for Alicia to avoid possible conflicts of interest that might occur.

28. a. The ethical concern is that the action is bribery.

29. b. A proper investigation is necessary for ethical purposes. This is to ensure that all sides of the situation are analyzed and that a solution can be found.

30. b. It is best for Ryan to talk with the women he works with. They can give him ideas on what he can do to improve his behavior when interacting with them.

31. c. You are responsible for reviewing all the new HR requirements. Therefore, you must use due diligence to be able to make sensible decisions.

32. a. Your business might have a conflict of interest policy that could keep something like this from working accordingly. You would have to review such a policy to determine if you need to change something in your operations.

33. d. You can use as many metrics as needed provided they analyze your business functions. This includes having enough employees on hand to handle the production.

34. b. Your analyst must identify your benefits.

35. c. A full analysis of your business data is necessary to identify what your business is doing.

36. c. You will have to check the rules yourself, although a separate party may be hired to assist you.

37. d. Each of these points can contribute to a positive environment to produce the best results in the workplace.

38. d. A lack of a work/life balance may make it harder for a business to function due to not knowing why employees are leaving your employ.

39. c. Risk mitigation is a process to keep negative effects from occurring.

40. a. An agency shop agreement is for employees who work for you but do not join a union but still have to pay union dues. This is to encourage the non-union people to eventually become union members.

41. a. A public policy exception is in effect when an employee who is wrongfully removed may be the victim of the company not following its public policies. This means that the fired employee has a legal case against the employer.

42. c. A person can receive unemployment benefits for up to 26 weeks if they are actively seeking new employment.

43. d. These reducing insurance costs. But you must ensure that you do not remove people without a reason to do so.

44. c. A health report can include the benefits received by the employee and if they are to move the benefits that they receive to another employer.

45. a. Inclusion is ensuring that all people have an equal say. Diversity will not be effective if you are not willing to allow everyone to get together in an inclusive environment and voice their opinions.

46. a. The competitive intelligence analysis process is a closer look at how well your business is working based on how it stands in the market. This includes looking at any possible changes to a local environment.

47. b. The mission statement is stating the purpose of the business.

48. a. Predominantly, the OECD includes companies from modern countries in Europe.

49. b. An involuntary separation occurs when a person is unable to continue. This could be the result of a long-term disability or a layoff, or, in many cases, a person might have died.

50. a. An oral contract is informal.

51. a. You have to have a sound reason or have just cause for removing someone from a position.

52. d. An ombudsman is responsible for being neutral and identifying the needs of both sides of a disagreement.

53. a. Restructuring is a process where a business is adjusted composition and layout of the business so that it becomes more profitable.

54. d. The actual deferral percentage or ADP is a measure of 401(k) plans. The key is to ensure that there are no discriminatory actions taking place between people who are being compensated and those who are not.

55. a. A benefit plan requires a person to pay for a benefit that will be used later. The policy will be paid out to the person at the time of retirement.

56. b. The defined contribution plan is the contributions being revealed, but it is unclear as to what the benefit will be to the person upon retirement.

57. a. A scatter diagram helps you review how two variables relate to one another.

58. b. The act states that the copyright will last for the life of the person who originally held the copyright followed by 70 years after that original period of time.

59. a. The act says that a copyrighted item for a piece of work for hire can be for 120 years from the date of creation or 95 years from the date of publication. The condition that expires first is the one that will be given copyright protection.

60. b. A classroom style for seating is people sitting in horizontal rows facing in one direction. The design ensures that people will be able to pay attention to the speaker.

61. d. A workforce analysis identifies the workforce by the department. This includes a review of each person in a department based on hierarchy and salary.

62. a. To overcome the stage of resistance is by ensuring the workers understand what the plan is and why changes are necessary.

63. c. A transformational leader is someone who will inspire people and motivate them to do more.

64. a. A reaction response is noticing how the information in question is being received.

65. d. A BARS review is a behaviorally anchored rating scale review. This identifies the behaviors that people engage in and to analyze how they are performing in their individual jobs.

SHRM-SCP Exam 1

1. What form of market differentiation is working with conformance standards?
    a. Service
    b. Channel
    c. Product
    d. Price

2. Porter's general strategy of a focus is the following:
    a. Providing specific services
    b. Having no-frills operations
    c. Being more unique in one's work
    d. Any of these could work

3. Diversification is a strategy for building a business that entails:
    a. Offering products to various types of people
    b. Selling new products in new markets
    c. Trying to sell old products in new markets
    d. Any of these can work

4. Which of these options is suitable for when you want to build your skills?
    a. Attend HR conferences
    b. Hire a mentor with more experience
    c. Ask people to challenge what you are thinking
    d. All of the above

5. What does it mean when your employees are purposely working slowly?
    a. Personal aggression
    b. Political deviance
    c. Production deviance
    d. Property aggression

6. What type of business operation occurs when the people in the work environment operate as investors but don't influence operations?
   a. Joint venture
   b. Sole proprietorship
   c. General partnership
   d. Limited liability entity

7. For what can you use the SMART model?
   a. Training employees
   b. Forecasting things
   c. Arranging goals
   d. Hiring people

8. What can be said about the Clayton Act?
   a. A strike cannot be broken by an injunction
   b. Organizational rights are available to workers
   c. Proper rates must be paid to people on occasion
   d. The best rules for work should be planned

9. What should be done regarding performance appraisal?
   a. Rank your employees
   b. Review the employees based on their most important tasks
   c. Use better samples to analyze the employees
   d. Decide future needs

10. Paid leave can be used for:
    a. Illnesses
    b. Maternity
    c. Funerals
    d. All of the above

11. The Pension Protection Act states that:
    a. Companies that fund retirement accounts should be held liable
    b. Retirement accounts are to be protected from possible losses
    c. The process of funding a pension should be transparent
    d. All of the above

12. The Sarbanes-Oxley Act is about:
   a. Protecting shareholders from accounting errors
   b. Stopping fraud among companies via full disclosures
   c. Protecting people from potential losses
   d. A and B

13. The Small Business Job Protection Act has done all but which of the following?
   a. Controlled tax rules for small businesses
   b. Defined minimum wage rules
   c. Established rules for how often people are to receive training
   d. Provided clear rules for how pensions are to be paid

14. What makes a goal different from a strategy in the workplace?
   a. There's no difference between the terms
   b. A strategy comes before a goal
   c. A goal is an end, while the strategy is how you get there
   d. A senior HR professional will plan a strategy

15. Which of the following may be interpreted as a chemical health threat?
   a. Bacteria
   b. Pesticide
   c. Fungus
   d. Virus

16. The Workforce Investment Act resulted in the following:
   a. Definition of what a mass layoff may be
   b. 60-days notice given before a closure
   c. Labor unions are to work with managers for training purposes
   d. Training centers should be planned to support the work that many people do in the workplace

17. Does union decertification ensure that employees still have the right to join another union?
    a. Yes
    b. No
    c. Depends on the union
    d. A time period is needed for waiting

18. What is a viable reason why a union might become decertified?
    a. It is too expensive to operate
    b. It is no longer useful
    c. It is too large
    d. The group is struggling to operate

19. What portion of a union is there a need to petition the NLRB for a vote on decertification?
    a. 10%
    b. 30%
    c. 50%
    d. 70%

20. The Weeks v. Southern Bell court case is critical for:
    a. Fighting gender-based discrimination
    b. Analyzing communication standards
    c. Controlling pay standards
    d. Deciding what is right for management standards in the workplace

21. The McDonnell Douglas Corporation v. Green case involves:
    a. Proving Title VII concerns
    b. Analyzing monopolies
    c. Blocking union activities
    d. Keeping workers from being able to strike

22. How many employees does a company need to be protected under Title VII of the Civil Rights Act of 1964?
    a. 5
    b. 15
    c. 50
    d. 100

23. What aspect of affirmative action is getting enough demographic information details on the labor market?
    a. Job group analysis
    b. Determining availability
    c. Comparing incumbency surrounding the availability
    d. Organizational profile

24. What is the most important issue about a cost-per-hire activity?
    a. Advertising becomes a burden
    b. You are ignoring some of the costs involved
    c. No distinctions are made between jobs
    d. Some things depend on outside economic factors

25. What are you doing when you are arranging the chairs for employee orientation in a grouping?
    a. Getting people ready for group work
    b. Having people watch a presentation
    c. Helping them to compare notes
    d. Planning questionnaires

26. Can a strike be illegal due to misconduct among those going on strike?
    a. Yes
    b. No
    c. Depends on how many people are involved
    d. If there is a dramatic threat involved

27. A hot cargo clause may be supported by people who are on strike. What would this mean?
    a. They demand better conditions in the work environment
    b. They refuse to handle work given to them by management that is unfair to unions
    c. There are concerns surrounding the ongoing management
    d. Workers want extra protection for their salaries

28. Is it legal for a group to go on strike due to a hot cargo clause?
    a. Yes, provided it hurts the union
    b. Yes, assuming the event is sensible
    c. No, it is not legal at any time
    d. A full review is required first

29. The Norris-LaGuardia Act states that:
    a. Yellow dog contracts are illegal
    b. People can conduct sit-down strikes
    c. Arbitration is necessary to end a strike
    d. Courts can demand that strikes end even if nothing is resolved

30. Are work slowdowns legal strikes?
    a. Yes, so long as standards are met
    b. Yes, provided that everyone participates
    c. No, the risk to the business can be too great
    d. No, the safety risk can be significant

31. What should your business be doing about testing employees?
    a. Schedule regular tests are needed
    b. You can select which employees you want to test
    c. People should be given a choice to be tested
    d. Drug testing is needed before you can offer employment

32. Regents of California v. Bakke states that:
    a. Non-union employees cannot be given union rights
    b. Arbitration can be enforced when interstate actions take place
    c. People should have the opportunity to refuse arbitration clauses if they find them to be unfair
    d. Quotas cannot be used to boost hiring standards

33. This form of budgeting requires you to review and plan every expense:
    a. Parallel
    b. Historical
    c. Bottom-up
    d. Zero-based

34. What does historical budgeting entail?
    a. Keeping tabs on all expenses
    b. Assuming expenses from prior years are carried over
    c. Analyzing any budget items that are to be forwarded elsewhere
    d. Noting any changes in how your budget is arranged

35. The ADA states that one of the following is not considered a major life activity:
    a. Hygiene
    b. Reading
    c. Sleeping
    d. Driving

36. A person is covered by the ADA if they have an impairment surrounding:
    a. Physiological conditions
    b. Cosmetic disfigurement
    c. Loss of functionality in one or more body systems
    d. All of the above

37. The Family Medical Leave Act states that you should provide a new mother with at least how many weeks of unpaid leave?
    a. 3
    b. 12
    c. 20
    d. 26

38. To qualify for the FMLA, a person must have:
    a. Worked for a company for at least a year
    b. Have logged 1,250 hours of work
    c. Have a pension program with the employer
    d. A and B

39. An HMO can help provide medical services to the employees in your workplace in exchange for:
    a. Monthly charges that vary by each month
    b. Favors for business services
    c. A fixed annual fee
    d. Contracts for development

40. A preferred provider organization is a provider of medical services for workers in your business. The PPO will offer:
    a. Reduced rates for services
    b. Limits on who you can visit for services
    c. The freedom to go anywhere for services
    d. A and B

41. The ERG theory from Alderfer states that the following is a relatedness need:
    a. Esteem
    b. Psychological
    c. Safety
    d. Self-Actualization

42. The ERG theory of motivation suggests all except one of the following stages:
    a. Growth
    b. Relatedness
    c. Existence
    d. Creation

43. In the Four Absolutes produced by Crosby, the process of achieving quality is prevention and not:
    a. Analysis
    b. Action
    c. Appraisal
    d. Measurement

44. Quality based on Crosby's Four Absolutes is:
    a. Conforming to requirements
    b. Out of goodness
    c. Working with appraisal
    d. Being able to keep expenses down

45. Martin v. Wilks states that:
    a. People can be denied due to certain quotas
    b. Race-based hiring practices may not be sensible
    c. People can be increasingly analytical over who is being hired
    d. None of the above

46. You are going to use analytical tools to decide what actions might affect the best possible improvements in your workplace. What particular tool is the best option for you to use in this situation?
    a. Pareto chart
    b. Histogram
    c. Stratification chart
    d. Gantt chart

47. You are trying to work with many employers to negotiate with others. What specific form of bargaining are you using?
    a. Integrative
    b. Parallel
    c. Multi-unit
    d. Positional

48. You might be assuming that negative behaviors in the workplace are brought upon by personal activities rather than the work environment. What are you experiencing in this situation?
    a. Nonverbal bias
    b. Questioning
    c. Conditional bias
    d. Fundamental attribution error

49. What can your HR department do to help fund your business actions?
    a. Acquire a loan from a bank
    b. Sell stock
    c. Get partners to help you by investing
    d. Look for government practices that can help

50. ERISA states that people who are involved with graded vesting practices have to be in a qualified plan:
    a. Now
    b. In a year
    c. In seven years
    d. At one's discretion

51. You need to conduct a SWOT analysis for your business. When is the right time for doing so?
    a. When adjusting policies
    b. When evaluating your business
    c. When reviewing your business environment
    d. When planning a new activity

52. A worker who gets $50,000 a year has a midpoint in one's salary range of $80,000. What would be the compa-ratio for the worker?
    a. 62.5%
    b. 75%
    c. 90%
    d. 160%

53. The Worker Adjustment and Retraining Notification Act states that:
    a. Expansions for a business must be voted upon
    b. Anyone who has to relocate must get help for the process soon
    c. Proper training is needed for those who are unemployed
    d. All workers must be informed in advance of any problems they come across

54. What type of business has to complete an EEO survey?
    a. A bank that offers bonds
    b. A school
    c. A small staff (less than 100 employees)
    d. A large staff (more than 100 employees)

55. Washington v. Davis states that:
    a. Laws that have discriminatory issues have to be changed
    b. People can create their own rules on how minorities can be treated
    c. There are no limits surrounding how people are to be cared for
    d. Laws can be interpreted as being racially neutral if they have no discriminatory intent

56. A person may be measured based on one's ability to be productive and active. What is this a measure of?
    a. Labor
    b. Return on investment
    c. Human capital
    d. Productivity standard

57. What can cause a performance analysis to fail?
    a. Unclear goals
    b. Stereotypes
    c. Seniority considerations
    d. People working on the reviews not trained

58. The Dilbert Principle is a concept in HR that involves:
    a. People being promoted to remove them out of the workflow
    b. People not receiving enough training
    c. People being tested on the wrong things
    d. Overstaffing

59. For how long should an OSHA form be held?
    a. 1 year
    b. 3 years
    c. 5 years
    d. Depends on the type of form

60. Which of these comparisons of the OSHA forms is incorrect?
    a. Form 300 – log of work-related injuries
    b. Form 300A – summary of work-related injuries
    c. Form 301 – incident report
    d. All are accurate

61. A union can choose to withdraw an election petition that would cause an election bar for six months. What is this known as?
    a. Blocking charge bar
    b. Prior petition bar
    c. Contract bar
    d. Withdrawn petition bar

62. The Weingarten rights state that employees who are being interviewed for an investigation have the right to:
    a. Silence
    b. Union representation
    c. Reschedule

d. Defer their work

63. Severance pay is given when a person:
    a. Leaves one's job
    b. Is unwillingly terminated
    c. Has legal concerns
    d. Cuts off union contracts

64. An election has been declined by the NLRB due to a collective bargaining agreement changing actions. What bar is this?
    a. Statutory
    b. Contract
    c. Blocking charge
    d. Prior petition

65. The Blake-Mouton Grid states that a Country Club entity has:
    a. More care for people
    b. More care for work
    c. Less care for people
    d. None of the above

66. The Blake-Mouton Grid states that a person in high authority or obedience is based on:
    a. Job performance
    b. Personal needs
    c. Neutral activities
    d. Union support

67. Flexible compensation is often preferred when paying the benefits that workers are owed because:
    a. The operating costs are low
    b. The compensation is based on the needs of the employee
    c. There is no risk of discrimination
    d. Such benefits are easy to distribute

68. Your business must fill out an EEO-1 report if you have how many employees:
    a. 40
    b. 60
    c. 80
    d. 100

69. Is the status of a person being a parent a protected class?
    a. Yes, for non-adoptive parents only
    b. Yes, for adoptive parents only
    c. Yes, for all parents
    d. No

70. What is a jurisdictional strike?
    a. A strike that occurs in a certain physical area
    b. A strike against a separate party
    c. A strike involving various suppliers or other outside groups
    d. A strike against work being moved to members of another group

71. What makes a defined benefit plan useful?
    a. Employees contribute to it on their own
    b. The benefits are protected
    c. Monthly benefits are given at retirement
    d. Such plans are more diverse today

72. A golden parachute can be given to an executive in the event of all but one of the following:
    a. Restructuring
    b. Takeover
    c. Retirement
    d. Lawful removal

73. A gap analysis is a comparison based on:
   a. Hiring
   b. Performance
   c. Finances
   d. Growth rate

74. Which of the following is not an example of a bottom-up communication plan?
   a. Intranet communication
   b. Staff meetings
   c. Open-door policies
   d. All-on-dock meeting

75. How is a matrix organization of management arranged?
   a. One manager working in many departments
   b. The manager varies based on the situation
   c. People can manage themselves at times
   d. Multiple lines of reporting managers

76. Which is an example of indirect compensation?
   a. Health insurance
   b. Flexible scheduling
   c. Choosing your own reward
   d. Job development

77. What is not necessary for discussions with an employee about ways to improve?
   a. Explain disciplinary points
   b. Talk about expectations
   c. Get a person to sign something
   d. Discuss the behaviors that are impacting their ability to perform well

78. What should a mission statement include?
    a. Strategic plans
    b. A statement of where the business stands
    c. Plans for the group
    d. A statement of values

79. An apprenticeship in the HR field could be given to those who are:
    a. Looking for a new job in a specific field
    b. Receiving on-the-job training for a position in the future
    c. Learning about the evolution of the field
    d. Planning activities for work

80. What makes a wildcat strike different from a typical strike?
    a. The strike occurs at random
    b. The strike is more aggressive in nature
    c. The union leaders did not approve of it
    d. The employees are not on board all the way

81. Which is the highest level of Bloom's levels of learning?
    a. Evaluation
    b. Application
    c. Knowledge
    d. Comprehension

82. The synthesis part of Bloom's levels of learning involves:
    a. Remembering info learned earlier
    b. Understanding facts
    c. Gathering information
    d. Making judgments

83. Which of the following points has nothing to do with understanding problem-solving actions?
    a. Interpretation
    b. Recognition
    c. Examination
    d. Differentiation

84. What can be interpreted as due process?
    a. Producing a bargaining topic
    b. Allowing the NLRB to monitor progress
    c. Working with union shop functions
    d. Respecting the legal rights owed to an employee

85. The Kirkpatrick model of training is:
    a. Identifying one's ability to learn
    b. Noting how well a person can handle business operations
    c. Reviewing how well training sessions are operating
    d. Measuring how well a person can gather data

86. Which of the following parts of the Kirkpatrick model is not included?
    a. Reaction
    b. Learning
    c. Behavior
    d. Response

87. There is a plan for people to be paid similar pay for jobs that have the same skill requirements. This is referred to as:
    a. Equal pay
    b. Pay equity
    c. Competence pay
    d. None of the above

88. The Equal Pay Act allows for exemptions for the following except:
    a. Merit
    b. Seniority
    c. Quantity
    d. Age

89. When should you pay a temporary employee for overtime?
    a. During the holidays
    b. If the person is an intern
    c. Never
    d. If you review the pay rate

90. Can paid vacation time go toward overtime pay?
    a. Depends on the amount of time
    b. Only during non-peak times
    c. Never
    d. Only if the paid vacation is approved ahead of time

91. A fiduciary is a person who establishes a relationship between a trustee and the:
    a. Ownership
    b. Beneficiary
    c. Organization
    d. Union

92. The Hay evaluation method entails an analysis of:
    a. A job
    b. A person
    c. A union
    d. A business enterprise

93. Can a person who lost a job due to downsizing receive unemployment benefits?
    a. If the business is large enough
    b. At all times
    c. No benefits are available
    d. Depends on the situation

94. A constructive discharge occurs when a person is removed from the workplace due to the work environment becomes hostile. What makes this discharge different?
    a. The hostile employee resigns
    b. The hostile employee is fired
    c. The other employee leaves
    d. A union head leaves

95. The Hay evaluation is based on:
    a. Writing skills
    b. Job title
    c. Performance
    d. None of the above

Answers to SHRM-SCP Exam 1

1. c. Product differentiation is considering the features of a product or the quality of what you are offering.

2. a. The focus aspect is working with very specific things that you want to highlight.

3. b. You can use diversification strategies to sell new products to different markets that you have not yet reached.

4. d. Each option allows you to expand your knowledge and challenge yourself.

5. c. Production deviance occurs when people work slower than usual on purpose. These people may be doing this to show they are unhappy with certain conditions or actions in the workplace.

6. d. A limited liability occurs when people are investors without influencing the daily operations in the workplace.

7. c. The SMART points are about planning goals in the workplace. This includes working with goals that are specific, measurable, action-based, realistic, and time-based.

8. a. The Clayton Act states that the free market needs to be protected against monopolies. Therefore, injunctions cannot be used by employers to prevent strikes.

9. b. The performance appraisal process identifies how well people manage different tasks in their job.

10. d. Paid leave is given to an employee who is experiencing dramatic life-changing concerns that might impact their ability to continue working. The terms for the paid leave may vary according to the situation.

11. d. The Pension Protection Act ensures that people will have funds for retirement.

12. d. The Sarbanes-Oxley Act states that there must be transparency in business reporting and that proper disclosures are provided and all accounting information is available.

13. c. The act outlines the financial functions for small businesses but doesn't dictate how the business is operated.

14. c. Goals are long-term objectives, and strategies are needed for the HR department to be effective.

15. b. Pesticides are chemicals that are used on lawns and other green spaces and are dangerous to those who are exposed to them.

16. d. The act states that proper training is required for all workers and employees. This is to ensure people can be more productive.

17. a. Decertification does not mean a person cannot join another union later.

18. b. In some cases, a union might no longer be needed because many of the needs of the workers have been met or are no longer relevant.

19. b. The NLRB needs 30% of the union members to vote to agree for the union to become decertified.

20. a. Gender discrimination cannot be used to eliminate a person from employment.

21. a. Title VII is a part of the Civil Rights Act that states that people cannot be discriminated against based on sex, race, religion, color, or national origin.

22. b. Title VII applies to businesses that have 15 or more employees, as well as groups that are supported by the government.

23. b. Determination of availability requires demographic information to be provided to people within certain groups. This is to ensure that hiring is fair.

24. d. There are too many outside factors that might influence the process of hiring the right people in the workplace.

25. a. The process is about ensuring that people are ready to work in general group activities.

26. a. Those who engage in illegal or potentially harmful activities might be at risk of putting others in danger.

27. d. A person is assigned the job of mediating a dispute between parties. That person is completely neutral and is not involved with either side of the dispute.

28. c. A hot cargo clause is used when workers refuse to handle goods or work given to them by an anti-union employer.

29. a. A yellow dog contract is a contract that states a person cannot join a union that is not connected with his employer. A worker has the right to join a union provided that union is active at their place of employment.

30. a. A work slowdown states that people continue to work, but they are not working to capacity and are doing the bare minimum.

31. b. Drug tests and other tests may be specifically ordered for employees who need to have the physical or mental focus to do their job properly and safely.

32. d. The court case focuses on universities, but this may involve businesses as well. Racial quotas cannot be used when deciding who is to be hired.

33. d. Zero-based budgeting involves justifying all your expenses.

34. b. Historical budgeting is used when you know the expenses because they were included in the budget in other years and will affect your business in the future.

35. d. Driving is not interpreted as a major life activity according to the ADA. Such activities include ones that are necessary for life like seeing, eating, sleeping, reading, thinking, working, and communicating.

36. d. The ADA states that all of these conditions are situations that might make it difficult for people to complete some of the tasks in the workplace.

37. b. A new mother or father can take unpaid leave for at least 12 weeks once every 12 months. An employee must provide at least 30 days' notice before approval is granted for this unpaid leave. The person does not have to take the leave, although it should be offered regardless.

38. d. The FMLA only allows for unpaid leave when the employee has a certain amount of experience with the employer.

39. c. A health maintenance organization can provide medical services to people through a series of supported medical providers. An HMO can be hired by an employer to provide services to the employees.

40. d. A preferred provider offers services at reduced rates and places limits as to who the employee can visit.

41. a. The ERG theory refers to existence, relatedness, and growth. Esteem is a part of relatedness. This may be interpreted as a streamlining of the hierarchy of needs that Maslow developed.

42. d. Creation is not a part of the ERG theory.

43. c. An appraisal is a consideration about how something might work. Quality is preventing certain things from happening.

44. a. The concept of quality is ensuring that proper standards for operation are enforced.

45. b. The court case states that there is risk involved with race-based hiring.

46. a. A Pareto chart shows a combination of bar and line graphs that illustrate the causes of a problem. The bars illustrate the causes, while the lines show improvements that may develop when certain causes are removed from the picture.

47. b. Parallel bargaining is a practice where a union will work with another employer to negotiate a better deal for the workers.

48. d. The fundamental attribution error states that personality cannot be the main focus of employment. Punishment does not resolve the issues that negative personality causes.

49. b. Issuing stock promotes the development of new actions in the workplace. The shareholders that buy the stock can earn dividends if the stock increases in value.

50. c. Graded vesting is allowing the funds for a project to be released gradually. Cliff vesting may also be considered, although a person would have to be vested in a plan within five years.

51. d. The SWOT analysis is about planning work, although this may entail evaluating the operations within your business and outside threats.

52. a. The compa-ratio is the person's salary divided by the midpoint and then multiplied by 100 to determine the percentage.

53. d. The act states that all workers must be given at least 60 days notice if a business is going to shut down operations. This is to give a worker the opportunity to plan for other employment.

54. a. A bank that provides savings bonds in the United States must complete the survey to confirm a company's hiring practices.

55. d. The court case ensures there are no problems arising regarding how people are hired or supported in the work environment.

56. c. Human capital is a measurement of the staff that produces the goods or services of a company.

57. a. A lack of clarity in the goals defined can make it harder for a business to stay active and operational.

58. a. The general principle is to ensure the workforce has the skills necessary to perform the work effectively.

59. c. All forms that are filed need to be held for 5 years after the end of the calendar year that the forms are for.

60. d. Each form identifies many concerns or concepts in the work field.

61. b. A prior petition bar is used when a union removes a petition for an election. This means that the NLRB will not hold an election and will bar the elections from occurring for the following 6 months.

62. b. The Weingarten rights report on how a person can have a union representative on hand to support the worker's needs when there are concerns about their employment history.

63. b. Severance pay is the pay that a person gets when their position is eliminated and that person is no longer necessary. Not everyone who is laid off will receive severance pay.

64. b. A contract bar states that the NLRB cannot allow representation in a unit handled by a contract until a 3-year limit expires.

65. a. The grid states that the Country Club mentality has a lot of support for the people, but it does not necessarily support the work involved.

66. a. The Obedience mentality infers that strict adherence to rules is needed for the job to be done correctly.

67. b. A person will have the option to choose from different benefits based on their needs or preferences.

68. d. The EEO-1 report of Title VII standards requires a business with 100 employees or more to comply with providing data on race, gender, and job category of the business.

69. c. All parents can be protected in accordance with EO 13152.

70. d. The strike may occur because the work in a situation is being moved to a different jurisdiction. This may be interpreted as being unfair to the workers.

71. c. The monthly benefits are given to the employee at retirement.

72. d. The golden parachute is named for the retirement package of immense bonuses given to executives. However, an employer who has just reason for removing someone from their position may withhold benefits.

73. b. The gap analysis considers the gap between the performance of the business now and where the business wants to be in the future.

74. a. An intranet is an internal communication between managers or executives.

75. d. Many line managers are responsible for gathering the data for managerial and organizational purposes.

76. a. Indirect benefits are benefits that are not monetary. Health insurance in this situation is such a benefit.

77. c. A signature can confirm that someone has received a review, but it is not as important as the other things listed in this question. A full discussion is necessary for the employee to know and understand what should be done in the future and what is expected.

78. d. The mission statement should be a few sentences in length. The statement is the general values that business supports.

79. b. An apprenticeship is allowing an employee to work in a different job in order to become proficient and move into that job in the future if the job is available.

80. c. A wildcat strike occurs as one section of the union is opposed to something in the workplace and initiates a strike. All the employees in the union will enter the strike regardless of the situation.

81. a. The levels of learning are creation, evaluation, analysis, application, understanding or comprehension, and knowledge or remembering.

82. c. Synthesis occurs when a person gathers enough information to propose unique ideas regarding what they are studying or working on.

83. a. You would use interpretation to apply certain things based on what problems you notice or how you're going to solve them.

84. d. Due process is the legal requirement to respect the legal rights owed to employees.

85. a. The Kirkpatrick model concentrates on how someone can learn and behave and then how results may be produced as necessary.

86. d. The Kirkpatrick model uses the steps of the reaction, learning, behavior, and results.

87. b. Pay equity is people being paid for work of the same value. This includes allowing men and women to have the same pay when their skills and job requirements are alike. This is not like equal pay, a concept where people are given equal pay for equal amounts of work.

88. d. People have the right to receive the same amount of money regardless of age.

89. c. Temporary employees are not eligible for overtime pay. Non-exempt employees who have been working for more than 40 hours in a week can get overtime pay. Working on a holiday is not included in this situation.

90. c. Vacation pay is not included in the overtime pay. Vacation pay is paid for at a separate schedule versus the regular pay. A person who completes regular work as scheduled will receive overtime if that person works with more than 40 hours in a week.

91. b. The fiduciary is a means of responding to the legal concerns and considerations that a business might hold surrounding its operations.

92. b. People are not evaluated in the Hay System; jobs are evaluated.

93. b. A person who loses a job due to downsizing can receive unemployment benefits because the job loss was not within their control. This only applies if the worker is an official employee and is not self-employed or working as a temporary employee.

94. a. The constructive discharge is when the discharge is caused by the employee's actions and that employee voluntarily leaves the job. This should improve the operation of the business.

95. d. The Hay System concentrates on considering a job based on its functionality in the workplace.

SHRM-SCP Situational Exam 1

1. Tom wants to produce a new HRIS review. What data can he use from the employee records he reviews?
   a. Cell phone numbers
   b. Home zip code
   c. Dental plan
   d. All of the above

2. After getting his information ready, Tom wants to implement his plan. What is his first step?
   a. Determine vendor requirements
   b. Identify project parameters
   c. Review software packages
   d. Determine requirements

3. Sonya is developing a new employee handbook to be used for reporting on specific data about how people function in the workplace. What should she be doing with her employee reports?
   a. Produce summaries of each procedure
   b. Identify historic information on processes
   c. Figure out alternative approaches
   d. All of the above

4. A warehouse is hiring extra people and will require some employees to stay in certain work assignments. What should HR do to ensure the changes are managed effectively?
   a. Explain changes to employees with a new project plan
   b. Allow the most experienced employees first dibs on choices
   c. Let senior executives decide what will work
   d. Let the employees discuss these changes among themselves

5. Michael is facilitating a merger between his American company and a company based in Australia. What should he do to ensure the cultures don't clash during the merger?
    a. Have a subordinate review the situation
    b. Plan meetings that include both companies to accommodate cultural differences
    c. Specify cultural differences
    d. Produce complaint forms so people can respond to the situation as needed

6. Michael is deciding to manage changes for a workable succession plan. This includes considering the skills of employees to decide on the succession order. What should be noticed in the files?
    a. Records on the skills and abilities of each person
    b. A list of the best people having one skill
    c. A review of everyone based on who could be given a promotion
    d. A listing of all things regardless of possible assignment

7. A company recently downsized due to competition and its difficult business plan. What should the HR organization do?
    a. Cost-justify training
    b. Work with many employees so they understand changes
    c. Review training
    d. Link development programs to the new organization

8. You are compiling recommendations for converting a matrix organizational structure in the HR department. What should be noticed?
    a. No reporting relationships are found
    b. Close monitoring is required
    c. Extra break-in time is needed
    d. A union will oppose the matrix structure

9. Proper disclosure is required for due diligence before a merger can proceed. What would you have to disclose?
    a. Accessibility standards
    b. Discrimination records
    c. Safety class info
    d. A budget used for overtime

10. Your business is going to downsize due to economic concerns. What is the best thing for you to do?
    a. Compare your plan to others
    b. Analyze your plan based on diversity
    c. Decide who will be impacted
    d. Prepare a written report on the effect of downsizing on your budget

11. You just noticed an employee has been stealing money out of the accounts receivable account in your workplace. What should you do here?
    a. Ask the person to give the money back
    b. Suspend the employee
    c. File a police report
    d. Initiate an insurance claim

12. A union is boycotting your business. What should you do in this situation?
    a. Negotiate with the union
    b. Take the union to court
    c. Explain to the public that the union is wrong
    d. Have the legal department in your business take care of the situation

13. You have been dealing with a union leader who has been abusive and disruptive. What should you do in this situation?
    a. Nothing
    b. Have a one-on-one discussion with the leader
    c. Suspend the leader
    d. Call the union president and ask how to resolve the issue at hand

14. You need to provide an FMLA a leave notice to your employer. How much notice should be given?
    a. 3 days
    b. 7 days
    c. 15 days
    d. 30 days

15. You want to identify the best possible leaders in a collaborative environment. What is the best type of test that you can use in this situation?
    a. Emotional intelligence
    b. Personality
    c. Psychomotor
    d. Work test

16. Your HR department has received complaints about the salary the CEO is earning. What should you do to promote fairness in the workplace?
    a. Determine the rewards versus long-term goals
    b. See that the plan is based on long and short-term goals
    c. Determine the objectives used for managing evaluations
    d. Review your company's culture

17. You are contemplating merging your business with another group that has a new technology that can provide benefit to you. What type of change is contemplated?
    a. Radical-reactive
    b. Incremental-reactive
    c. Radical-anticipatory
    d. Incremental-anticipatory

18. You are planning a gain-sharing action in the workplace. What would be your greatest concern?
    a. High-performing employees will be frustrated
    b. It becomes harder for new workers to handle certain tasks
    c. There's no incentive for anyone
    d. It becomes harder for money to be shared

19. Your business is not meeting particular diversity initiatives. What is the best thing you can do to incorporate diversity?
    a. Establish a new diversity initiative
    b. Encourage employee referrals
    c. Review discrimination claims over hiring
    d. Analyze your work staff

20. An employee has brought his W-4 form to you and says that he is not subject to payroll withholding taxes because he says he always pays his taxes directly. What should you do?
    a. Give the worker a Form 1099
    b. Ask the accounting department for help
    c. Tell him that everyone on staff is required to have monies withheld for taxes
    d. Ask for a W-10 form

21. One of your employees is angry and has insulted you on her social media page. What applies to this situation?
    a. Ask her to remove the post
    b. Do nothing
    c. Threaten legal action against her
    d. She is protected from prosecution or retaliation by law

22. A worker wants to have her SSN unlisted in her profile out of fear that her SSN will be stolen. What is the best solution for you to consider here?
    a. Remove the SSN from her records
    b. Keep the SSN but don't record it on her records
    c. Tell her the SSN is needed for tax purposes
    d. Say that the SSN is needed for census reports

23. A company wants to have updated information on the race and sex details of the people in the workplace. Is this sensible?
    a. Based on FLSA requirements, that information is required
    b. No one needs to provide this information
    c. Only select people can offer this information
    d. It is illegal to ask for this information

24. The work week has been chosen to start on a particular day of the week. Can the HR manager change this?
    a. Yes
    b. No
    c. Depends on the time of the year
    d. The work week starts on a Sunday

25. You have a fifteen-year-old worker who has been given a position with you as a summer job. You are asking him to work for 9 hours on Saturdays. Is this legal?
    a. Yes, based on all rules
    b. No, based on local rules
    c. No, based on federal laws
    d. The answer varies based on whether school is in session or not

26. You have a 17-year-old working in the workplace who is interested in driving a forklift or another large machine because another employee is unable to come to work. Can you legally let him drive the machine?
    a. Yes
    b. No
    c. Train him first
    d. Give him a test beforehand

27. Jeff is working 45 hours a week. How many hours should he be paid for?
    a. 45
    b. 47.5
    c. 50
    d. 55

28. Your payroll clerk is handling the payroll in the workplace. You might have a new worker, but you are uncertain if that person should be paid extra for his skills. Is it legitimate for that person to be paid more than what others in the same job are being paid?
    a. There are no restrictions
    b. Everyone is paid according to how long they have worked in that job
    c. All workers receive the same pay
    d. Conduct a review to determine how much more he should be paid

29. You are planning to implement a new life insurance policy for everyone in your workplace. However, you can add a self-insured policy if you wish. What should be considered when getting this to work right where you are?
    a. No restrictions are necessary
    b. Review the welfare benefits involved
    c. Make your decision based on the LIBPA
    d. Check your state laws first

30. You are asking for an I-9 form from a new worker. You are given a driver's license to confirm one's identity. What should be done next in this situation?
    a. Ask for another document as per the I-9 instructions
    b. Review the SSN
    c. Ask for a passport
    d. Make sure that person files for an SSN in the next 30 days

31. A worker in your business has suddenly fallen ill while on the job as is in critical condition at the hospital. What should you do in this situation?
    a. Call the hospital and get the insurance company involved
    b. Report the illness to the OSHA
    c. Ask what he was doing at the time of his injury
    d. Contact the worker's spouse or next of kin

32. Susan feels that she does not require the same ethics training program at her workplace every year because she feels she knows everything about what she needs to do. What should be said to her to encourage her to keep working on ethics training?
    a. Say nothing, as there are no real legal requirements
    b. Explain that federal laws require annual training
    c. Talk about state laws
    d. Explain that refresher courses are needed

33. You noticed a sinkhole in your office parking lot. What should you do?
    a. Review the quality of the sinkhole
    b. Create a guard over the sinkhole
    c. Alert others to the sinkhole right away
    d. Both b. and c.

34. Your office has a number of sharp materials that have to be handled regularly. These include some needles. What should you do these sharps after you are finished with them?
    a. Break off needles before disposing of them
    b. Triple-wrap the needles before disposing of them
    c. Use an appropriate container that has been properly labeled
    d. Add sharp materials to a red-wrapped container

35. A worker in your office doesn't want to be subjected to a urine test for drugs. He feels that this is a violation of his privacy. What should happen next?
    a. Let him contact a lawyer to be exempt from taking the test
    b. Remove the worker from his position
    c. Allow him to select when he wants to be tested
    d. Use an alternative testing process

36. You are developing a flexibility plan for employees for vacation leave. One thing you can do is to:
    a. Add vacation time
    b. Reduce advance notices
    c. Assign leave times according to seniority
    d. Give leave dates to supervisors

37. You are being told to prepare the OSHA 301 incident report for your workplace. What should you do?
    a. Distribute copies within seven calendar days
    b. Hand out a segment about the case
    c. Provide a copy within 24 hours
    d. A and B

38. Do you need compliance officers in the workplace to obtain an inspection warrant for someone to enter the work site?
    a. Recommended
    b. Unnecessary
    c. Is a requirement by law
    d. Can have many details

39. You are planning a training method to understand the problems in the workplace. This includes noting how well the workplace is running. You can talk about possible solutions that may work with a third-party. What type of training should be used?
    a. Demonstration
    b. Vestibule
    c. Facilitation
    d. Conference

40. An HR manager is acquiring a new company. What is the HR manager going to avoid considering?
    a. Economic factors
    b. Who will be a successor
    c. Layoffs for duplicate roles
    d. How viable the acquisition is

41. An EAP counselor is planning a review of a sexual harassment claim. What should the counselor do?
   a. Have the employee report the harassment to the HR department
   b. Report the harassment to the HR department
   c. Reach the EEOC for help
   d. Contact the plant manager to learn more about what is happening

42. A company is closing down, but it is not giving 60-days notice stating that there will be a closure. Why is this legal?
   a. The HR manager doesn't have to explain anything
   b. The company has more than 100 employees
   c. The company only has 40 employees, and they are part-timers
   d. The company has employees who work fewer than 4,000 hours in a week in total

43. One of your exempt workers is going to be at home for half a day due to weather hazards. What are you required to pay that worker?
   a. Half a day of pay
   b. A full day of pay
   c. Time and a half
   d. Nothing

44. You are closing your workplace early due to extreme weather. What should you pay your exempt employees?
   a. Half a day of pay
   b. A full day of pay
   c. Time and a half
   d. No payment

45. A group that works with a union has a complaint against only one subcontractor, but everyone is going to strike anyway. What type of strike or picketing action is taking place?
    a. Common situs
    b. Alter ego
    c. Organizational
    d. Double-breasting

46. You are reviewing the candidates who have applied for work. You are concerned about negligent hiring. What is the best solution for you to consider when reviewing the candidates?
    a. Background check
    b. Reference check
    c. Polygraph test
    d. A and B

47. Twenty percent of the workers at a business who are represented by a union have signed a petition to start a deauthorization process against the union. What should the NLRB do in this situation?
    a. Deny the petition
    b. Allow for an election to happen
    c. Have a hearing between the union and the employees
    d. Decertify the union's relationship with the workers

48. Mary says she is unable to work on Sundays for religious reasons. What should you do in this situation?
    a. Explain that a religious request is not professional
    b. Deny the request due to the fear of this creating a hardship
    c. Determine if your other employees are going to make their own adjustments to their schedules
    d. Approve the request

49. You may come across a situation where ADA and FMLA laws interfere with some rules about workers compensation. What should you do in this case?
    a. Honor whatever rules benefit the employee the most
    b. Decide which law is most applicable
    c. Use the law that is the strictest
    d. Use the law that benefits the business the most

50. Robert feels he was discriminated against because his employer did not respect his request for Sundays off for religious reasons. How much time does he have to file a discrimination charge with the EEOC?
    a. 150 days
    b. 180 days
    c. 365 days
    d. Right after the discrimination takes place

51. You are using a bell curve to rank the employees according to how well they function at work. How should you rate your employees?
    a. As high as needed
    b. As low as needed
    c. With a majority in the middle of the curve
    d. With a majority at both the front and end of the curve

52. A union wants automatic deductions to be taken from the workers' paychecks and paid the union. What should the union do in this situation?
    a. Ask the NLRB
    b. Ask the employees their opinion
    c. Allow individual employees to do this on their own
    d. Let the members agree to the deduction

53. An audit is being conducted in the HR department to review the compensation provided to employees. Which of the following does not have to be analyzed?
    a. HR layout
    b. Compensation details
    c. Wage compression
    d. Healthcare expenses

54. HR is conducting an audit regarding employee relations. What might have to be assessed?
    a. Diversity practices
    b. Turnover details
    c. Conflict resolution practices
    d. All of the above

55. You are contemplating approving a successor employer. What does the NLRB state that is necessary?
    a. Ensuring the operations can continue
    b. Reviewing particular activities to ensure they are consistent
    c. Reviewing specific operational practices
    d. All of the above

56. You are planning an HR audit based on recruitment processes. This includes distinct affirmative action policies. What functional area are you going to focus on?
    a. Labor relations
    b. Organizing HR functions
    c. Managing risks
    d. Planning your workforce

57. You want to confirm that sex-specific policies are preventing women who are pregnant or planning to become pregnant to be in contact with certain harmful chemicals and other compounds in the work environment. What law can be used?
    a. EEOC
    b. WHD
    c. HHS
    d. DOL

58. A person is asking for leave as her child is being deployed by the military. However, her child is not ill. What should be done?
    a. Reject the leave
    b. Accept the leave
    c. Ask for USERRA leave
    d. Give the employee extra time off work

59. Your scorecard is being reviewed and you are told to work with a balanced review. What is the best thing to do?
    a. Align the work based on a strategy
    b. Add priority to certain subjects
    c. Measure the progress
    d. All of the above

60. You have an employee who has resigned from his position in the middle of the week. What should be done regarding his pay?
    a. Pay him for what he worked
    b. Pay him for the week
    c. Have him on a different schedule
    d. Cover his duties

61. You have a person in the workplace who has a disabled family member. COBRA coverage may be provided to the worker. How long can this be used?
    a. 12 months
    b. 18 months
    c. 24 months
    d. 29 months

62. You are uncertain as to whether a worker is an independent contractor or an official employee. Who can you contact to determine the answer?
    a. IRS
    b. DOL
    c. EEOC
    d. WHD

63. You are attempting to make the workplace more organized. What can you do in this situation?
    a. Plan a job evaluation
    b. Review internal equity
    c. Plan BLS analysis
    d. Use a factor comparison

64. What should you provide to a person who is about to be laid off?
    a. WARN notice
    b. Job listing help
    c. Outplacement
    d. Unemployment office referral

65. You want an employee to fill out an I-9 form. When should that person do it?
    a. 5 days before starting a job
    b. The day the employee starts working
    c. Upon the agreement for the job contract
    d. Based on the employer's discretion for the content

Answers to SHRM-SCP Situational Exam 1

1. d. The employee records should include information on any benefits, pay details, and contact information.

2. d. The business' requirements should be determined first, followed by identifying project parameters, a review of software packages, and then an analysis of what the vendors need.

3. a. The summaries in the employee handbook will ensure that the employees understand what they need to do to complete their work tasks.

4. a. Allow the employees to speak with you about how the situation is changing and what can be done to manage certain actions.

5. b. It is easier for people in the workplace to understand how to manage integration when they talk with each other about their needs and how those concerns can be facilitated.

6. c. You need information on the skills of the employees and how well they can handle particular activities. This includes ensuring that those people in the workplace know what is expected.

7. d. Development plans are needed to identify how certain actions are aligned and how the work is to be planned based on certain initiatives and plans that a workplace wants to use and follow.

8. c. It often takes some time for experienced workers to get used to some of the things they will be doing. Allow the people in the workplace to get used to the changes.

9. b. There is a potential for certain liability concerns to impact the cash flow. You'll have to review the discrimination records in the workplace to determine if there are any liabilities that have to be addressed.

10. b. You will have to review how your business changes its functions based on the Age Discrimination in Employment Act. This is to ensure there are no unfair selection choices being made when downsizing.

11. c. Any theft of money should be seen as a criminal act that requires the police to be contacted.

12. a. Negotiation is the best solution to review the grievances that people have and how those problems can be resolved.

13. d. You are unable to discipline a person for their activities while representing a union. Therefore, you need to talk with the union president about what needs to be done to resolve the issue.

14. d. You need to provide 30 days' notice before the leave is granted.

15. a. The emotional intelligence of a person is the ability of a person to complete certain tasks.

16. d. Corporate culture often is a review of the history of your company. You might have to analyze the quality of the work being produced.

17. a. A radical-reactive approach is a major change due to the response to a major event taking place.

18. a. Gain-sharing is when everyone makes the same contributions to a plan. This can be frustrating for high-performing workers as they might feel that their efforts are not being appreciated.

19. a. A diversity initiative may include new goals to ensure representation in the workplace.

20. c. A worker will be subjected to all the major taxes that have to be withheld. People cannot opt out because they want to file their own tax reports.

21. d. The worker should be protected by the National Labor Relations Act. Although the worker is unhappy, most online postings are protected actions and should not be a problem unless her posts are negatively influencing the company or the workforce.

22. c. The SSN is required by the IRS to ensure that proper tax records are kept.

23. a. The FLSA states that information on race and sex are required for all workers.

24. b. The FLSA states that an employer must designate a particular day of the week as the start of the work week. The day cannot be changed as a means of facilitating faster activities and actions.

25. c. Federal laws state that a person who is 15 years of age or under cannot work more than eight hours in a day regardless of the time of year.

26. b. Workers under the age of 18 are not allowed to operate heavy machinery due to the risks involved.

27. b. The FLSA states that any hour worked beyond 40 hours in one week should be interpreted as time and a half. That is, the 5 hours should be paid as 7.5 hours.

28. c. The workers who were in the job before the new person in the workplace started should receive the same pay. Therefore, the new worker should be paid at the same rate as the other workers regardless of when they started work.

29. b. Welfare benefits should be analyzed.

30. a. You have the option to ask for another document according to the I-9 instructions, although you only need one.

31. b. It is critical to report the injury to OSHA within 8 hours of the incident to ensure that the details of the injury are recorded.

32. d. You have the right to require training provided that the training is regularly updated and includes behavioral standards that are critical for the workforce to perform the work and to do so safely.

33. d. It is critical to take precautions to prevent people from being hurt at work. You must also contact the proper authorities to resolve certain problems before they become worse.

34. c. The container for sharp object disposal should be labeled and approved for use based on the Needlestick Safety and Prevention Act. The proper notices are posted on the container stating the use.

35. b. Drug testing is mandatory in most industries. You will have to ensure that people comply with the testing processes and that those who refuse are declined employment.

36. Since vacation pay is optional, the employer could reduce the advance notice requirement.

37. a. A copy of the data needs to be delivered within 7 days.

38. a. It is recommended that a compliance officer provides an inspection warranty before a person enter the job site.

39. c. Facilitation is a practice where many employees work together to resolve the same problem. A facilitator is a third-party hired to help resolve the problem.

40. d. The viability of the acquisition is not critical for the HR department as much as the ability to manage accounting functions.

41. a. The EAP is the employee assistance program. The program encourages the worker to provide the details of the incident to the proper authority, particularly the HR department in this situation.

42. c. The WARN Act states that a warning should be provided when there are more than a hundred full-time employees in the workplace. In the situation described, there is no need for the HR department to adhere to the WARN Act because the workers are not working full-time and there are not enough employees in this situation.

43. b. The FLSA states that an exempt employee must receive pay their work based on scheduling and you cannot give less than a full day's pay to that person as long as the reason for his absence is reasonable.

44. b. Even if the business closes early due to weather, the employees should be paid for a full day of work.

45. a. Common situs picketing is a situation where picketing occurs at other employers' locations even though the union has a grievance with only one employer.

46. d. A reference check confirms a person's past experiences related to their employment. A background check could reveal offenses or accusations of wrongdoing outside their employment.

47. a. You need to ensure that 30% of the workforce has signed the petition. If less than 30% has signed, the NLRB would have to decline the petition.

48. c. Ask other employees if they are able to work the hours that the employee is unable to work.

49. a. Both the FMLA and ADA are responsible for the protection of employees. Since the two laws may intersect with each other, you have to choose the law you feel may be the most beneficial or accommodating to the employee who needs the assistance.

50. b. The EEOC states that a discrimination charge has to be filed within 180 calendar days of the issue happening. This may be extended to 300 days depending on local laws.

51. c. You'll need to review the bell curve with the averages involved falling in the middle part.

52. c. The employee should be asked for their opinion.

53. a. You can use an HR audit to identify the functions of the business along with rewards or benefits given to the employees.

54. d. The HR audit process has to be a thorough review of everything that is going on in the workplace.

55. c. The operations should be reviewed based on the actions and legal concepts that have to be used when designing a smart plan for the operation.

56. d. Your planning can include everything from reviewing recruitment to a supply analysis.

57. a. The EEOC enforces the Pregnancy Discrimination Act.

58. b. The leave terms include dealing with concerns surrounding an immediate family member who may be sent away on military service.

59. d. You can use the balanced scorecard to communication functions and align work strategies and structures. You can also determine which tasks are going to be the most important for the employees.

60. a. The FLSA states that the employee should be paid for the work done. This means that the days that the person did not work should not be paid.

61. d. The COBRA coverage may be extended from the standard 18-month period by 11 more months depending on the situation.

62. a. The IRS can identify whether a person is an employee or a contractor.

63. c. A Bureau of Labor Statistics review can help you to be aware of the external wage information.

64. d. You can refer the work to the unemployment office.

65. b. The I-9 form should be completed on the first day of employment.

SHRM-SCP Exam 2

1. How long would it take for you to devise a mid-range plan developed?
   a. Three months
   b. Six months
   c. One year
   d. Two years

2. What type of pay would be provided to an employee who has to be sent home due to an office being overstaffed for the day?
   a. Call-back pay
   b. On-call pay
   c. Shift pay
   d. Reporting pay

3. Call-back pay is given to a person being asked to return to the workplace:
   a. Before one's allotted time for work
   b. After one's allotted time for work
   c. When a person works a holiday
   d. A and B

4. On-call pay is paid for:
   a. Emergency work
   b. Extra work
   c. Volunteer efforts
   d. New training efforts

5. What law states that an employee cannot demand extra pay for the commuting time?
   a. Commuting Compensation Act
   b. Portal to Portal Act
   c. Fair Labor Standards Act
   d. Davis-Bacon Act

6. The behavior portion of the Kirkpatrick training evaluation model states that a person should be reviewed based on:
   a. How well that person handles new skills on the job
   b. Whether a person is a visual or auditory learner
   c. How that person responds to training
   d. The impact of the work

7. What activities are included in the training process while in the learning stage of the Kirkpatrick system?
   a. Brainstorming
   b. Role-play
   c. Group discussion
   d. All of the above

8. What is the first thing to be aware of when conducting a training program?
   a. The results that come out of the training
   b. How people respond to training
   c. The changes in behavior that people put in
   d. Any unique attitudes that people hold surrounding their work

9. How old should a person be before they are assigned tasks or asked to handle materials that have been identified as hazardous?
   a. 16
   b. 18
   c. 21
   d. 25

10. A seamless organization is when there is:
    a. Lack of turnover
    b. No hierarchy
    c. Multiple managers
    d. A number of executives

11. OSHA requires all but one of the following when it comes to preventing injuries in the workplace:
    a. Fire prevention plan
    b. Sanitation system
    c. Safety rules posted
    d. Emergency action plan

12. Which of these is not an example of a pull factor that might influence how a business operates?
    a. Government policies
    b. Strategic control
    c. Declining barriers for trade
    d. Shrinkage in some markets

13. Which of these is not a push factor for how a business can operate?
    a. Globalized supply chain
    b. Trade agreements
    c. International recession
    d. Working to enhance your image

14. What makes an upstream strategy for HR different from a downstream one?
    a. Upstream points entail things made at the local level
    b. Managers make the decisions
    c. Strategies for how far things can go
    d. Points for working with many tasks of value

15. A multi-domestic strategy to operate your business would include this attitude:
    a. A high need for local responsiveness
    b. A low need for local responsiveness
    c. A high need for global integration
    d. A and C

16. What makes an international strategy for operations distinct?
    a. It is domestically focused
    b. You are exporting some products to select countries
    c. Not many links between headquarters and subsidiaries
    d. All of the above

17. When you choose remote locations for having access to vendors and supplies, what strategy are you employing?
    a. International
    b. Global
    c. Transnational
    d. Multi-domestic

18. What does Maslow's hierarchy of needs state workers need first?
    a. Physiological satisfaction
    b. Self-actualization
    c. Safety help
    d. Social access

19. What can inhibit the growth phase of a life cycle?
    a. Lack of response
    b. Excess rules
    c. Lack of communication
    d. Outsourcing

20. The Immigration Act of 1990 focuses on the following:
    a. Changes rules for how many immigrants a business can hire at the most
    b. Increasing the number of immigrants that can enter the United States every year
    c. Reviewing how people are to be monitored when entering the country
    d. Lists limits on what countries can allow people to emigrate to the United States

21. What makes the H-1B visa important for employers to consider when looking at immigrants who want to be employed?
    a. Entails temporary employment
    b. Focuses on specialty tasks
    c. Works for people from any country
    d. All of the above

22. Which of the following is not featured in the Scanlon plan?
    a. Identity
    b. Competence
    c. Functionality
    d. Benefit-sharing formula

23. What can be a concern about following the Scanlon plan?
    a. It may not motivate workers
    b. It may not get people to be involved
    c. There is too much emphasis on individual approach to work
    d. The process can become unwieldy if not handled correctly

24. The gross profit for your business is calculated by taking the cost of goods and:
    a. Subtracting it from the sales revenue
    b. Subtracting it from the profit
    c. Adding the liabilities for your business
    d. Reviewing how much is distributed to the employees

25. What is the main point of a Six Sigma analysis?
    a. How many errors you find in the workplace
    b. How complicated your work routines are
    c. How many experienced people are in the workplace
    d. A and B

26. What would a Black Belt in Six Sigma indicate?
    a. Operates as a mentor for project teams
    b. Reports issues to Green Belts
    c. Selects projects
    d. Provides training to new members

27. What makes a Master Black Belt different from a regular Black Belt in the Six Sigma process?
    a. The Master can create new tasks
    b. The Master focuses on the new culture in the workplace
    c. The Master is responsible for implementing changes
    d. A and B

28. What analytical strategy should you use to review a relationship between the production of the workforce and revenues?
    a. Ratio
    b. Trend analysis
    c. Scatter plot
    d. Linear regression

29. Faragher v. The city of Boca Raton states that:
    a. Employers cannot be held responsible for how their employees behave
    b. Sexual harassment cases are covered by Title VII
    c. Psychological damages can occur when there is a hostile work environment
    d. A hostile team environment can be implied in a harassment case

30. A Family and Medical Leave Act ruling mentions key employees being eligible for help. What is a key employee in this situation?
    a. Someone who leads others
    b. People who cannot be easily replaced
    c. Managers or executives
    d. Employees with high salaries when compared with others in your field

31. Does the Family and Medical Leave Act require a business to allow a key employee to return to their old position when they return to work?
    a. Yes
    b. No
    c. Depends on the industry
    d. Depends on how long the issue is good for

32. What appears at the beginning of Selye's General Adaptation Syndrome analysis?
    a. Alarm
    b. Resistance
    c. Homeostasis
    d. Exhaustion

33. When does the panic zone appear in Selye's General Adaptation Syndrome?
    a. After resistance
    b. After exhaustion
    c. After breakdown
    d. After homeostasis

34. In the Selye model, when are people at the greatest level of threat?
    a. Resistance
    b. Breakdown
    c. Homeostasis
    d. Alarm

35. A person may be refused worker's compensation due to an injury caused by a fellow co-worker. The concern is the:
    a. Fellow servant rule
    b. Assumption of risk
    c. The doctrine of contributory negligence
    d. None of the above

36. According to the Pregnancy Discrimination Act of 1978, pregnancy should be assumed to be:
    a. A disability
    b. An injury
    c. An illness
    d. None of the above

37. When should you conduct a realistic job preview?
    a. When you need to find a candidate who meets all the standards of the job
    b. When there's a high selection ratio
    c. When recruits have access to job data
    d. When unemployment rates are high

38. What form of job training can be interpreted as a passive method?
    a. Vestibule
    b. Presentation
    c. Seminar
    d. Case study

39. What type of patent is not recognized by the United States Patent Act?
    a. Design
    b. Structure
    c. Utility
    d. Plant

40. Which of these patents will last the shortest length of time according to the United States Patent Act?
    a. Plant
    b. Design
    c. Utility
    d. They all last the same length of time

41. A 401(k) requires pension contributions that are:
   a. Defined
   b. Fixed
   c. Variable
   d. Mandatory

42. A 401(k) employer-provided contribution plan is for:
   a. Governmental employees
   b. Retired persons
   c. Minors
   d. Nonprofit institutions

43. What makes a 401(a) plan different from a 401(k) plan?
   a. Contribution is voluntary
   b. The work is tax-free
   c. Taxes are variable
   d. The employer determines the contributions for a 401(a) plan

44. A utility patent will protect the creation of a new or improved:
   a. Machine
   b. Process
   c. Product
   d. All of the above

45. What makes a Quick Win project distinct in the process improvement?
   a. A new process is established
   b. The effort requires extra help from many groups
   c. The problem is in one department
   d. The process works in increments

46. Which of Juran's steps for quality improvement should occur first?
   a. Set goals
   b. Create awareness for the need to improve
   c. Offer training
   d. Organize the work in question

47. What should be done at the end of Juran's quality improvement process?
   a. Keep score
   b. Convey results
   c. Make annual reviews
   d. Recognize the people who worked on the task

48. A unionized work environment will often utilize what particular type of compensation plan?
   a. Incentive
   b. Performance
   c. Seniority
   d. Membership

49. Job pricing is an analysis of a job. This includes looking at:
   a. The description
   b. The title
   c. How fast a person can move up
   d. Any specific efforts one might put in

50. Job pricing requires you to match survey jobs to internal jobs based on:
   a. Titles
   b. Descriptions of jobs
   c. Age limits
   d. Salaries

51. A market gap in a job will be:
   a. Adjustments that a person must make to reach a job
   b. What the pay difference is between different tasks
   c. How many people might be asked to complete certain jobs
   d. A and B

52. This measurement rate involves a review of the number of new employees versus the total number of people in the workplace:
    a. Turnover
    b. Succession
    c. Replacement
    d. Ascension

53. Who signs off a job description questionnaire according to the Hay System?
    a. The job holder
    b. A supervisor
    c. Management
    d. All of the above

54. Which of the following cannot be said about a job evaluation?
    a. It is scientific in nature
    b. It compares tasks
    c. It judges the person who is working
    d. It is heavily structured

55. What is used when the Hay System is reviewed to confirm a job?
    a. Ability
    b. Seniority
    c. Skill
    d. Accountability

56. What is a major reason why so many management programs in the workplace might fail?
    a. Lack of ISO 9000 support
    b. Not noticing why change is valuable
    c. Focusing too much on core objectives
    d. Micromanagement throughout too many places in the organization

57. In what working environment are you more likely to experience a tuberculosis outbreak?
    a. Restaurant
    b. Gas station
    c. Child care center
    d. Senior living center

58. Feldman states that people are likely to confirm the expectations that they have prior to hiring during which stage:
    a. Acquisition
    b. Change
    c. Encounter
    d. Anticipation

59. Immigrant visas may be provided to people who enter the United States based on:
    a. Who applies first
    b. Work experience
    c. Nationality
    d. All of the above

60. What is not one of the three aspects of McClelland's needs theory?
    a. Achievement
    b. Affiliation
    c. Power
    d. Security

61. A manager is expected to recognize how employees are motivated. This includes looking at factors such as:
    a. Money
    b. Respect
    c. Image
    d. All of the above

62. A person who wants to achieve more in the workplace may be motivated by:
    a. Regular feedback
    b. Solitude
    c. Comfort with one's earnings
    d. Being able to handle work that is familiar

63. According to rules established by the Office of Federal Contract Compliance Programs, where can you go to find details on the ethnicity of an employee?
    a. Birth certificate
    b. Census form
    c. A person's own report
    d. You might have to make a personal judgment

64. You can establish a clause in the collective bargaining agreement based on people being asked to join a union within a certain time period. What type of clause may be established at this point?
    a. Contract administration
    b. Union shop
    c. Closed shop
    d. Maintenance of membership

65. What should you do to get people to keep from being overwhelmed from excess information during the orientation process?
    a. Review the positives involved with the job
    b. Give out supplementary material to your employees
    c. Use one large meeting instead of several smaller ones
    d. Stop extensive discussions

66. An executive order surrounding employment processes could be declared and sent to a Federal Register so it can be reviewed before it officially becomes law. How long before it can officially become law?
    a. 30 days
    b. 60 days
    c. 3 months
    d. 6 months

67. Which of the following is a form of indirect compensation?
    a. Performance bonus
    b. Leave of absence
    c. Variable compensation
    d. Perquisite

68. Could a heroin addict be interpreted as a disabled person based on the ADA?
    a. It depends on their physical functionality
    b. In all cases
    c. In no cases
    d. It depends on if that person is receiving treatment

69. One form of arbitration may be used to allow the two parties in the negotiation to agree to a decision established by a third-party. What is this form of arbitration?
    a. Binding
    b. Ad hoc
    c. Constructive
    d. Compulsory

70. Research can find the difference between trained and untrained employees by using:
    a. Statistical power
    b. Selectivity
    c. Marginal difference
    d. Statistical significance

71. The Davis-Bacon Act is concerned with:
    a. Child labor
    b. Overtime pay
    c. Minimum wages
    d. Government employment

72. A style used to increase work efficiency is by:
    a. Giving instructions
    b. Noting effects
    c. Talking about competitors
    d. All of the above

73. A delegating style of leadership is followed when you want your employees to:
    a. Feel more confident in what they are doing by accepting more responsibility
    b. Obey your decisions
    c. Hear your ideas
    d. Determine how to do their jobs themselves

74. How does a seller type leader do to have others accept his decisions?
    a. Explain the costs
    b. Talk about why these decisions are useful
    c. Plan unique tasks to implement the decisions
    d. Offer instructions to make the most of those decisions

75. What is the greatest risk involved with an assumption?
    a. The risks depend on the department
    b. You might have less profit realized
    c. It may be incorrect
    d. You are exercising due diligence

76. What does AWOL in a job report mean?
    a. Absent without letting management know
    b. Absent without leave
    c. Average weekly overtime
    d. None of the above

77. Oncale v. Sundowner Offshore states that Title VII covers:
    a. Same-sex harassment
    b. Misleading content
    c. Issues based on religion
    d. Sexual insults

78. An S-shaped curve in the learning process states that a person is going to learn by:
    a. A sudden moment of realization
    b. Knowing what might work in a situation
    c. Getting better returns over time
    d. Reaching a peak

79. How long can it take for a person to attain a plateau when learning something new?
    a. It depends on the learner
    b. About a month
    c. After the basics are taught
    d. Depends on the subject matter

80. A self-directed study allows a worker to do the following:
    a. Analyze the work plan
    b. Communicate with others within the group
    c. Determine the rules
    d. Identify trends

81. Blended learning is a combination of what forms of learning?
    a. Audio and video learning
    b. Classroom and computer learning
    c. Working with new and historic contexts alike
    d. Working with many instructors

82. What would be an example of a virtual training session?
    a. Driving lessons
    b. Training with sample customers
    c. Completing analytical tests
    d. Flight simulator

83. What can be reviewed in the self-assessment process when training an employee?
    a. Values
    b. Interests
    c. Strengths
    d. All of the above

84. Career development requires a review of many trends. What can be studied in this situation?
    a. Changes in the industry
    b. Changes in a culture
    c. Analysis of the market
    d. Knowing your goals

85. A late-career development will include:
    a. Using existing skills
    b. Planning for retirement
    c. Life considerations
    d. Teaching younger people about certain tasks

86. When would a person be more likely to make a shift in career direction?
    a. Midcareer
    b. Late career
    c. Early career
    d. Organizational stage

87. A project lead will have to report to a manager who then reports to the:
    a. CEO
    b. Director
    c. VP
    d. Tech officer

88. Nontraditional employment is a concept in the HR field that involves:
    a. People working in jobs traditionally held by other demographics
    b. Temporary work
    c. Individual responsibilities
    d. People who have many jobs

89. What would be a reason why people work multiple jobs?
    a. To increase their earnings
    b. To have extra experiences
    c. To plan for retirement
    d. A and B

90. What things can a leader do to take care of him/herself?
    a. Balance work and home life
    b. Adapt to different cultures
    c. Put their own needs above everyone else's needs
    d. All of the above

91. An inventory is a way of measuring a person's particular skills. The score on an inventory is compared to:
    a. Rules for operation
    b. Ideas for making tasks easier
    c. Norm groups
    d. None of the above

92. A bonus may be interpreted as a:
    a. Benefit
    b. Form of compensation
    c. Perk
    d. All of the above

93. In order to produce a reward strategy, it must:
    a. Reflect your personality
    b. Be cost-effective
    c. Work according to your client's preferences
    d. Focus on loyalty

94. What do people want from their pay schedules?
    a. Security
    b. Frequency
    c. Details
    d. Flexibility

95. Establishing equity in the workplace depends on:
    a. Fairness
    b. Neutrality
    c. Cost-effectiveness
    d. Personal approaches

Answers to the SHRM-SCP Exam 2

1. d. A short-range plan should encompass less than a year. A mid-range plan is for about two years. A long-range plan will cover three to five years.

2. d. Reporting pay is applied when an employee reports for work and is then sent home without penalty or punishment.

3. d. Call-back pay is applied when a person is subjected to extra working hours that are beyond what was scheduled. The terms of the pay can vary based on the employer and the standards set for compensation.

4. a. Emergency tasks in the workplace can be sudden concerns that require extra workers and someone has to come in at the last minute. Extra pay may be given to those workers.

5. b. The Portal to Portal Act states that a person cannot request payment for commuting time.

6. a. The behavior segment focuses on understanding how a person changes their actions due to the training received.

7. d. The learning step involves how a person handles the training in question. This includes understanding how their knowledge has increased.

8. b. The response should be reviewed based on how receptive people may be when taking care of particular tasks in the workplace

9. b. According to the Secretary of Labor, a person who is 18 years of age can be given tasks that entail activities that have been deemed hazardous.

10. b. A lack of a hierarchy is a sign of a seamless organization. This means that there are no restrictions on what a worker in the workplace can handle.

11. b. A sanitation system is recommended, but it is not demanded by OSHA.

12. d. A pull factor refers to something that might prompt people to move forward with certain tasks in the workplace. Shrinkage in a market is not a

pull factor, although the potential for a market to expand is something that incites people to take action in some way.

13. c. A domestic recession will have a greater effect than an international one. The domestic issue may push a business to take certain actions.

14. b. An upstream effort requires the manager to make decisions on the alignment of the workforce or the development of an organization. This includes looking at how knowledge is to be shared.

15. a. A multi-domestic strategy is used by a business to find markets and adapt to local interests.

16. d. An international strategy involves all products and services being developed in the home country. The items are then sent out to different markets around the world.

17. c. The transnational strategy involves remote locations being the suppliers and vendors. There is a direct link between the headquarters and all the subsidiaries that the company is working with.

18. a. The physiological needs that a person has include food, water, and shelter. A person needs to get to those needs met before focusing on other aspects of improving their life.

19. c. Improper communication can make it harder for a business to handle general growth and operations.

20. b. The act allows for extra people to enter the United States every year. This includes visas to be made available to people who are coming into the country to work.

21. d. An H-1B visa allows a person to stay in the country for three years and can be extended to six years. This also requires the person to have the skills necessary for the job they will be doing in the workplace.

22. c. The Scanlon plan focuses on cooperation, identity, competence, involvement, and sharing the benefits.

23. a. The lack of motivation is critical. Some people might not have enough experience or might have too much experience.

24. a. The gross profit is calculated by subtracting the cost of materials from the sales revenues.

25. d. Six Sigma focuses on reviewing the errors that develop in an operation. You would have to review the complications in your system and find ways to keep those errors from being extensive in the work environment.

26. a. A Black Belt is higher-rated than White, Yellow, and Green Belts. The Black Belt has advanced Six Sigma experience and can report to a Master Black Belt.

27. c. While a Champion selects tasks, a Master Black Belt implements the changes.

28. d. A linear regression looks at how two variables relate to one another.

29. d. A difficult team environment only has to imply harassment.

30. d. A key employee is defined as a person who is in the top 10% in terms of salary.

31. b. The key is to ensure that a business will not experience economic harm due to a person being unable to work. The business has the right to fill a position if necessary. The FMLA states that a business should make all attempts to have the worker return to their old position if possible. New fill-ins can be hired on a temporary basis.

32. c. Homeostasis is the stage that occurs before a change takes place. This is the norm that people are used to experiencing.

33. b. The panic zone happens when people attempt to manage a change. As people start to notice the change, they become tired and less resistant, although there might be that one last attempt to get things to return to normal.

34. a. The resistance stage occurs after the alarm stage and is the time when the most worry about the change occurs.

35. a. The fellow servant rule states that a person cannot receive compensation if a fellow co-worker causes an injury. However, the rule does not have to be the only factor to make decisions, as sometimes there might be malicious intent.

36. a. Pregnancy is to be considered a short-term disability. Therefore, the pregnant woman should receive disability benefits for a determined time.

37. a. A realistic job preview reviews the possible recruits that might be hired. The key is to ensure that only those who absolutely meet the standards for that job are interviewed.

38. b. A presentation involves a person being asked to listen to what is being presented. Therefore, the worker is not necessarily going to be interacting with others as much as one would with the other three forms of training.

39. b. A structure patent is not a type of patent that the United States Patent Act notices. The other three patents are respected though.

40. b. A design patent lasts for 14 years, while both a utility and plant patent can last for 20 years.

41. a. A person will be able to define the contributions being made here. This might entail a person making contributions based on a percentage of whatever income one might earn. In some cases, the contributions may entail a person getting the contributions to be matched.

42. b. The 401(k) plan is for retirement.

43. d. An employer will determine the contributions to be made in the 401(a) plan. The 401(k) plan allows the worker to decide what he/she wants to contribute to their retirement plan.

44. d. A utility patent is for a particular item designed to produce a result or benefit in the workplace.

45. c. The concept of the Quick Win task is working with something that can be handled in a few moments and can involve only one department.

46. b. Establishing awareness is the absolute first step. After that, a business must set goals and organize the operations to reach those goals.

47. c. The annual review is used to determine if any specific changes have to be made to the operation of the business.

48. c. Seniority is important as it may be used to set the wages of an employee.

49. a. The job description is examined to reflect the skills needed for the job.

50. b. The description of the new job should match the descriptions of the survey jobs and internal jobs.

51. a. The market gap focuses on the changes that might take place in the work environment.

52. d. The ascension rate considers the new people being hired. A high rate suggests that a business might be over hiring.

53. d. The Hay System states that the job description should be signed by the employee, the supervisor or management.

54. a. A job evaluation is comparative, judgmental, focused on the job, and has a strict structure. The evaluation is not scientific, nor is it absolute.

55. d. Knowledge, accountability, and the ability to solve problems are critical aspects of managing the work. The accountability in this situation refers to how well other people in a business can rely on a person.

56. b. The changes in the workplace are critical to managing for success and for allowing a business to grow and thrive.

57. d. Tuberculosis is an airborne disease. It could be easy for a senior living center to develop a TB infestation due to a large number of people working closely with one another.

58. c. The encounter stage is when people first meet one another to discuss plans for work. This stage may entail a closer look at what might go on when trying to hire a person and make one's work operate well enough.

59. a. Immigrant visas may be subjected to limits. Therefore, it is critical for people to get into the workplace as soon as possible before the limit on the number of visas being offered is reached.

60. d. The needs theory states that people want to be powerful, but they also want to be associated with other people. Security is not a direct part of the process, although it could be a useful side effect of the work.

61. d. Motivation is what propels people to work. Without motivation, nothing would be done.

62. a. Regular feedback provides information about how the rules are being accepted or challenged.

63. c. A worker can provide information about their ethnicity if they are asked and are willing to answer.

64. b. A union shop agreement is when people join a union within a specific time interval. The interval should be for about 30 days.

65. b. Supplementary material can be provided to people so they can get more information on whatever they are studying.

66. a. There is a 30-day period between when the executive order is established and when it can be made official and considered legal.

67. b. A leave of absence is considered indirect compensation and is granted by management in certain situations. The worker on leave will not receive pay.

68. d. A person who is going through treatment for addiction may be interpreted as being disabled, albeit temporarily.

69. a. A binding arbitration occurs through with a third-party who decides the outcome and a plan to implement the ruling. The arbitrator acts like a judge.

70. a. Statistical power refers to identifying trained and untrained employees.

71. c. The Davis-Bacon Act involves minimum wages.

72. a. Efficiency in the workplace can be increased by giving instructions.

73. a. Delegating tasks can shift responsibilities and increase a worker's self-confidence.

74. b. The seller is a master persuader.

75. c. An assumption might not necessarily be correct. You would have to look beyond assumptions and complete your own due diligence to prove your assumptions true or false.

76. b. AWOL means that a person is absent without leave; they are absent without having been granted permission to be away from work.

77. a. The case states that it is possible for people to engage in sexual harassment against others of the same sex.

78. a. The S-shaped curve for learning is when a person has a sudden realization of information they already know or had forgotten that they knew.

79. a. The plateau in learning is the point at which there doesn't seem to be further learning or an increase in skills. This could come about gradually or suddenly...

80. b. The self-directed study allows people to interact with others in order to clarify some questions about the study material.

81. b. Classroom and computer learning can be combined together to make it easier to learn.

82. d. A flight simulator is an example of a virtual training program in a simulated environment that is as realistic as possible.

83. d. Self-assessment should be used to identify the factors in one's work environment that might influence their efficiency and productivity.

84. a. Certain changes in the industry may influence what one wants to do in the way of career development.

85. b. The late-career period of one's work will involve planning for retirement.

86. a. A midcareer change often occurs when a person worries about the work being satisfying and considers a career change.

87. b. The director may report to a VP, who then reports to a CEO.

88. a. An example of a nontraditional employer who hires a woman as a referee at professional football games.

89. d. Working multiple jobs often increases a person's earnings, but can also be to expand their competency in the workplace by working at other tasks.

90. a. Self-care is doing what is necessary to have a positive attitude and find a balance between home and work.

91. c. You would compare your skills to norm groups.

92. b. A bonus is a type of compensation.

93. b. A reward strategy must be cost-effective and produce a positive attitude within the workforce.

94. a. Security is what pay schedules can give employees.

95. a. Establishing equity in the workplace depends on all decisions being fair.

SHRM-SCP Situational Exam 2

1. Your company is attempting to manage a project management lifecycle and keep the content intact. What should be noticed?
   a. Approval has to be secured
   b. The task is temporary
   c. You will have to review the overall scope and schedule of the work
   d. The task will be integrated into your organization after it is finished

2. You are aiming to conduct an affirmative action plan analysis that focuses on reviewing positions based on race and gender within each department. What type of analysis are you conducting?
   a. Workforce
   b. Job group
   c. Availability
   d. Utilization

3. Your business is planning a new change initiative to identify how to change and adjust its functions. What would be the first step for you to look at when getting in touch with your employees?
   a. Engage your workers
   b. Overcome the resistance
   c. Communicate the change
   d. Reinforce any changes

4. You are asking your employees to analyze their training. The evaluation you are asking is to review the effectiveness of the instructors involved, the material in question, and the presentation format. What type of evaluation is this?
   a. Reaction
   b. Learning
   c. Behavior
   d. Analysis

5. You are conducting a thorough appraisal of your business to evaluate the functions of each position and individual tasks. The ratings will identify a range of what someone does. What is the rating scale that you would use?
   a. Paired comparison
   b. 360-degree review
   c. Critical incident report
   d. BARS analysis

6. You are interviewing many people in the workplace to see how training has influenced attitudes. What is this analysis called?
   a. Results
   b. Learning
   c. Behavior
   d. Assimilation

7. Your business has experienced a natural disaster. Is this an exception of the WARN standards?
   a. Yes, in all cases
   b. Yes, based on the event
   c. No, in all cases
   d. Review your company's specific policy first

8. Joseph is learning a new task quite well, but after a while, he is unable to handle his work well. What type of learning curve is Joseph experiencing?
   a. S-shaped
   b. Plateau
   c. Negatively accelerating
   d. Positively accelerating

9. You have an architecture print you have drafted. Can you use the Copyright Act of 1976 to it protected?
   a. Yes, in all cases
   b. Yes, based on the draft
   c. No, in all cases
   d. Review your company's rules

10. A company's employees are unhappy with the current actions of their union. They have signed a decertification petition. The employer has received this petition. What can be said about the process?
    a. The employer cannot do anything
    b. The employee can remove the workers from the union
    c. The NLRB must review the petition
    d. The employer is complicit in the process and therefore can do nothing

11. Susan said to her employer that her presentation is in the public domain and is therefore safe to work with. What should the employer do here?
    a. Review the copyright data
    b. Look at fair use standards
    c. Determine the age of the information
    d. Look at the presentation

12. You want legal protection for something you are working with. What type of patent covers physical appearance?
    a. Ornamental
    b. Design
    c. Utility
    d. Plant

13. A company is contemplating decertification of a union in response to the employees' petition. What percentage of the people in the workplace should have signed this petition?
    a. 20
    b. 30
    c. 40
    d. 50

14. A company that has filed a petition for decertification has not been ready to negotiate with its union on a collective bargaining agreement. When can the company submit its decertification petition?
    a. In 30 days
    b. 12 months after the election of the union
    c. 24 months after the election of the union
    d. You'll have to avoid submission of the petition

15. Another company that has filed a similar petition for decertification has already negotiated a collective bargaining agreement with the union that it is trying to avoid the request of the members. When can the decertification petition be submitted?
    a. 12 months after the CBA was ratified
    b. 24 months after the CBA was ratified
    c. About 60 to 90 days before the third anniversary of the ratification
    d. 60 to 90 days before the CBA expires

16. Facebook acquired the Instagram and WhatsApp programs as a means of expanding its footprint in social media. Facebook is engaging in:
    a. Vertical integration
    b. Monopolistic processes
    c. Deductive purchases
    d. Horizontal integration

17. Ikea is contacting a metal company in Finland to produce the metals that are used for the company's tools to assemble their furniture products. What is Ikea doing when engaging that Finnish company?
    a. Strategic positioning
    b. Competitive advantage
    c. Vertical integration
    d. Horizontal integration

18. A lockout has started based on a bargaining impasse. Is this legal?
    a. For up to a year
    b. In all cases
    c. In no cases
    d. For less than a month

19. Ryan talks to his employees about changes to some of their healthcare benefits, but the employees are not happy about this. Ryan contacts his personal assistant to see what can be done. What type of thinking is Ryan using?
    a. Subjective logic
    b. Objective logic
    c. Inductive reasoning
    d. Deductive reasoning

20. A manager is being told that an employee engagement survey that was conducted is not working as well as it should. The manager feels that the survey was not as effective as it should have been. What is the manager using when considering the concerns about the survey's effectiveness?
    a. Subjective logic
    b. Objective logic
    c. Deductive reasoning
    d. Inductive reasoning

21. Your team is planning an improvement process based on the Kaizen model to identify how waste can be lessened. What would be the best material to use in this process?
    a. Fishbone diagram
    b. Pareto chart
    c. Process flow chart
    d. General bar chart

22. What does a Kaizen model review involve to determine countermeasures in the workplace?
    a. Comparative analysis
    b. Affinity diagram
    c. Cost of quality report
    d. None of the above

23. You are conducting a strategic planning process. What will be the last point to consider?
    a. What is your goal?
    b. What is your mission?
    c. How will you accomplish your goal?
    d. How will you know when you have reached your goal?

24. Michael is exempting an employee from a difficult task because he has not been absent from any scheduled work in the last year. What type of operant conditioning is Michael using?
    a. Extinction
    b. Positive reinforcement
    c. Negative reinforcement
    d. A and C are both essentially the same thing

25. Your employer is providing group term life insurance to its members. The terms exceed $50,000 per employee. What will your employer be subjected to in the process?
    a. Sarbanes-Oxley provisions
    b. Tax deductions based on the income
    c. OBRA rules
    d. All of the above

26. Concerted activity is being planned by employees in the workplace. How many employees are going to be used?
    a. At least 5
    b. At least 2
    c. All employees are entitled to protected activities
    d. Bargaining units

27. A labor union is in the middle of a dispute with a company. The union is preventing suppliers from having access to the company's plant. What should the suppliers do?
   a. Stay out of the issue
   b. File a ULP charge
   c. Bargain with the union
   d. Stop providing supplies to the company

28. A company is in the middle of a strong period of momentum and is trying to manage its succession plans while avoiding bureaucracy. What is the best effort to use?
   a. Maturity
   b. Decline
   c. Introduction
   d. Growth

29. The NLRB just certified a new union. However, that union is unable to arrange an election for the next year and will have to wait before it can conduct such an election. What is this practice known as?
   a. Prior petition bar
   b. Certification year bar
   c. Blocking charge bar
   d. Election bar

30. A union member is not paying his union dues. Could he be fired from his job?
   a. Yes, for a year
   b. Yes, at any time
   c. No, not at any time
   d. No, provided he pays his arrears

31. A union member is engaging in anti-union activities. Could he be fired from the union shop?
    a. Yes, following a full review
    b. Yes, assuming there is a significant threat involved
    c. No, as long as he pays his dues
    d. No, he would have to give an explanation for what he is doing

32. A bargaining unit is operating in a right to work state. About half of the employees are paying their union dues. What should be the consequences?
    a. Everyone in the bargaining unit will receive union representation
    b. Non-union members have to pay a portion of the union dues
    c. All employees are represented regardless of whether they are in the bargaining unit or not
    d. A union shop must be established with dues being automatically deducted from the employees' pay

33. Tony has learned a skill in his old line of work that has carried over to the new situation that he finds himself in. What is this process of how Tony is working called?
    a. Generalization
    b. Transfer of training
    c. Carry-over
    d. All of the above

34. You are working on a new job evaluation process to review the values of certain jobs based on skills required, the knowledge involved, the effort one must put in, and the working conditions that will be experienced. What is this particular evaluation called?
    a. Benchmarking
    b. Hay System
    c. Ranking
    d. Point-factor

35. You are interviewing a candidate and accepting many of their responses not so much as fact, but rather because the answers are socially acceptable. What would this consideration be called?
    a. Reasoning bias
    b. Cultural noise
    c. Manipulation
    d. Central tendency

36. Your employees engaged in illegal activity, but you are being held liable for their actions. On what standard are you being charged?
    a. Quid pro quo
    b. Constructive discharge
    c. Vicarious liability
    d. Employer liability

37. You want to enhance the quality of your ongoing ethics analysis program. What should you do to get the program up and running?
    a. Review the legal applications of the ethics you want to use
    b. Include the executive management in the process
    c. Review the code of conduct rules in the workplace
    d. Talk to your employees about the dangers associated with illegal activities

38. Your workplace has some employees who are under the age of 21. Can you remove them from a pension plan?
    a. It depends on their ages
    b. In all cases
    c. In no cases
    d. It depends on the length of time they have been an employee

39. Your workplace has some employees who have been working for you for less than a year. Can you remove them from the pension plan?
    a. It depends on how many hours they work in a week
    b. In all cases
    c. In no cases
    d. It depends on if they are union members

40. One of the positions in your workplace has become vacant, and now you are looking for a way to fill that position. What should you do?
    a. Determine the budget for recruitment
    b. Determine the compensation you will provide
    c. Post an ad for the job opening
    d. Review any possible changes needed to the job description

41. Before you make a job offer, you have to consider many factors about the candidate. What is the first criterion to consider?
    a. Review how the candidate communicates
    b. Check to make sure the candidate does not have a criminal record
    c. Ensure the candidate is physically capable of handling the job
    d. Determine if the candidate is authorized to work in your country

42. A candidate is complaining about being denied membership to a particular segment in the workplace. The candidate has a legitimate complaint in this situation due to:
    a. Unfair practice
    b. Disparate impact
    c. Adverse impact
    d. Disparate treatment

43. A startup has planned a new project that requires certain skills. After a year, the startup is planning to test the employees' performance. The test shows a positive change in skills. What does this mean?
    a. Changes in one's skills can cause positive changes in performance
    b. Better-performing employees will have higher test scores
    c. A variance in skills and job performance should be noted
    d. A statistical difference may be noticed between the programming training and the performance

44. A group at a business is taking part in active responses to disasters in the community. What is this an example of?
    a. Near-shoring
    b. Corporate governance
    c. Strategic planning
    d. Corporate responsibility

45. Mark has been working in the same position in his workplace as Tim. While Tim has been working for less time, he is earning more than Mark for the same work. What is this an example of?
    a. Benchmarking
    b. Equal Pay Act violation
    c. Equity theory analysis
    d. Wage compression

46. A large company that does not have union membership is shutting down a plant in the next few months, thus resulting in the loss of a few hundred jobs. Seniority may be used to decide which employees will receive a severance package and which employees will not. What law is to be used in the process?
    a. ADEA
    b. FLSA
    c. NLRA
    d. WARN

47. You are testing the general coordination of a worker to determine how that person can handle certain physical movements. What type of testing should be used?
    a. Personality test
    b. Aptitude test
    c. Cognitive ability test
    d. Psychomotor test

48. You are trying to reduce employee turnover. What should you do in this situation?
    a. Plan exit interviews to see why people are leaving the company
    b. Review your competitors to see what they are paying
    c. Increase the employee benefits
    d. All of the above

49. Your business has 100 employees and has contracts of over $50,000. You want to provide material to a particular business. Based on EO compliance, you must:
    a. Plan an affirmative action program
    b. Use suppliers that have been approved by the group you are working for
    c. Recruit more people
    d. Plan employment opportunities for specific people

50. You just accepted the resume of an applicant who is qualified for a position, but you are not going to interview them because they have a mental disability. This is based on previous records about that person. What are you violating what when you are doing this?
    a. OWBPA rules
    b. ADA rules
    c. Discrimination laws
    d. You are actually protecting yourself against negligent hiring in this case

51. You are asking a job candidate about resolving a conflict between two lower-level employees in the workplace. What type of question is this?
    a. Behavioral
    b. Hypothetical
    c. Structural
    d. Situational

52. You are actively planning a needs assessment. What should you avoid looking at in this situation?
    a. Reviewing what the goals for your training
    b. Determining the cost benefit
    c. Determining that the training is a solution to a particular problem
    d. Considering the legal requirements for specific types of training

53. A company hiring drivers will have its employees take practical driving tests. What type of validity is this?
    a. Criterion
    b. Content
    c. Curricular
    d. Construct

54. You are training a grouping of employees about how to avoid sexual harassment. You are then evaluating the employees to see if they understand the implications of their actions. What type of evaluation are you doing?
    a. Reaction
    b. Behavior
    c. Learning
    d. Results

55. Troy has been working for his employer for less than 12 months. He has recently been ordered to active military service for nine months. He should then be reemployed after the service period is finished. What does the USERRA state about Troy's military service?
    a. He will have met the 12-month FMLA employee requirement
    b. Each month that a person is actively serving in the military can be considered a month of employment with the company
    c. He will have worked for his employer for more than a year after his service
    d. All of the above

56. Your HR department is developing new programs to allow for a line of succession in the workplace. What will this practice involve?
    a. Benchmarking
    b. Needs assessment
    c. Collective bargaining
    d. Management buy-in

57. A worker scored 50% on his pre-test before being employed. After a few months of employment, they scored 60% on a new test. The training has increased the worker's knowledge of how much?
    a. 83%
    b. 20%
    c. 10%
    d. 120%

58. Carlos says that he received a promotion based on luck, but his manager says that Carlos was rewarded for the work he has done and this led to the promotion. The manager gave Carlos a top grade for his work. What type of bias is this?
    a. Opportunity
    b. Recency
    c. Primary
    d. None of the above

59. You are arranging for enough protective equipment for your workers based on OSHA standards. What do you not have to supply?
    a. Prescription safety eyewear
    b. Non-specialty protective footwear
    c. Flame-resistant clothing
    d. All of the above

60. Stuart requires a hearing aid for his work. Is this a sensible work accommodation?
   a. It depends on the intensity of the hearing loss
   b. In all cases
   c. In no cases
   d. You have to let the manager decide

61. A military veteran who is working for you needs a prosthetic leg following a significant injury while serving overseas. Can this prosthetic be considered a valid accommodation?
   a. Yes, specifically for veterans
   b. Yes, can work for all people
   c. No, not for anyone
   d. No, this would have to be determined based on the quality of the material

62. You are being encouraged by a foreign official to accept their business. You have to say that you cannot accept payment from an official, particularly if that person is trying to engage in some form of illegal activity. What law should you state when suggesting you cannot accept payment from that foreign official?
   a. Equal Employment Opportunity Act
   b. Fair Credit Reporting Act
   c. Foreign Corrupt Practices Act
   d. None of these laws

63. You are operating a construction company. Do you need to keep records on injuries and illnesses based on OSHA rules?
   a. Yes for all situations
   b. Yes for significant concerns
   c. Not for minor events
   d. Never

64. You are running a freight company with five employees. Do you need to keep records on injuries and illnesses in accordance with OSHA rules?
    a. Yes for all situations
    b. Yes for significant concerns
    c. Not for minor events
    d. Not in all cases

65. A person in the workplace was diagnosed with a work-related injury by an outside physician. Do you have to record the event?
    a. Yes
    b. Review the amount of time the worker will miss work
    c. Determine the extent of the worker's injury
    d. No

Answers to SHRM-SCP Situational Exam 2

1. b. Your task is temporarily based on how you will initiate the work, how you will plan and execute the task, and what you will do to control to process before everything is closed.

2. a. A workforce analysis process is a review of the work environment in each department.

3. b. There will be resistance at first. You have to explain to your workers what makes your efforts valuable.

4. a. A reaction evaluation identifies how well the people in the workplace were able to respond to the task. You are reviewing reactions based on the training provided.

5. d. A behaviorally anchored rating scale or BARS review considers the many behaviors that people might engage in.

6. c. A behavior review determines how well a person is responding to a training practice. This includes looking at how well a person has learned and if that person's behaviors are going to change based on that new knowledge.

7. c. A natural disaster is an exception to a WARN report. Other exceptions to a WARN report include unforeseeable circumstances that may negatively influence your business or cases where a business is faltering and is unable to remain stable for any reason.

8. b. The plateau curve states that a person might start to learn things quickly, but after a while, they will have gone through the maximum effort needed to handle the tasks and to improve.

9. a. You can use copyright to confirm that the architectural print is designed by you.

10. b. An employer cannot refuse to work with a union if the majority of employees in the workplace already agree to support that union. However, the employer can refuse to work with a union if the employees refuse the work in question.

11. c. The content of the presentation should be analyzed based on how old it is. A public domain work can entail anything that was published in the United States before 1923 and any works that were produced beyond the life of the author plus 70 years.

12. b. A design patent considers the appearance, while an ornamental patent considers what may be added to a different task or option you want to use.

13. b. At least 30% of the people in the union need to establish a petition. After this, the rest of the union members will be able to vote to dissolve the relationship with the union.

14. b. A petition may not be filed for a decertification vote for a year after a union wins an election. Petitions may not be filed during the first three years in a collective bargaining agreement either. A 30-day window is allowed for the petition, although the rules will vary based on the situation.

15. c. A 30-day window allows people to file a petition to initiate a decertification vote. The effort works about 60 to 90 days before the expiration date of the CBA or on the three-year anniversary of the CBA, whichever period comes first.

16. d. Horizontal integration occurs when a company acquires another company that is in the same industry.

17. c. Vertical integration occurs when a company acquires material that is required to make the tools needed for production.

18. b. A lockout can be employed due to the issues surrounding the bargaining stalling. This would work for most situations, although it may not be used for federal situations.

19. d. Deductive reasoning is a process where logical reasoning is being used to investigate the actions first to determine the results.

20. d. Inductive reasoning is an action that starts with the results and works back to the details of the actions that caused the results.

21. a. A fishbone diagram illustrates many of the steps that occur in a process. You can create a detailed fishbone diagram to determine which steps are excessive and may not be necessary. After this, you can establish a plan to cut down on the waste and to make your business more efficient.

22. a. A comparative analysis will determine the problems that are occurring in the workplace and how intense the situation may be.

23. d. The last question you need to consider is where your business will go and how will it progress.

24. c. Negative reinforcement is eliminating actions that are not positive.

25. b. The value of the particular insurance that is being offered should be examined based on the amount paid to each employee. A total of over $50,000 per employee must be reported as taxes for Medicare and Social Security.

26. b. You need at least two people to participate in such an action.

27. b. A ULP charge should be filed with the NLRB, as this is a secondary boycott. The Taft-Hartley Act states that secondary boycotts are to be prohibited. Such a boycott involves a union telling a neutral employer to stop doing business with another company due to an ongoing labor dispute.

28. a. Maturity involves a business having its profits and assets established in the current market. This is to ensure that regular operations and business efforts are to be supported.

29. d. An election bar is imposed when the NLRB is not going to hold an election. It may take about a year before the election bar can be removed.

30. b. A person who refuses to pay union dues can be fired by the union shop because of pressure from the union in question.

31. c. The anti-union activities can vary, but the only anti-union activity that would be considered grounds for being removed from the union shop is if that person refuses to pay union dues.

32. a. Fair representation is the point of the employee's grievance. Representation is all people in the bargaining unit are to be supported regardless of whether or not they are members of a union.

33. d. All three of these points are practically the same. A person is carrying over their training from one place to another work to perform their tasks.

34. d. A point-factor evaluation considers how well a person completes a task based on how well they know the job, the skills and responsibilities they have, the working conditions involved, and the effort of the employee.

35. b. Cultural noise involves a person providing sensible and conventional answers. These answers may be accepted and not disputed.

36. c. Vicarious liability is a situation where you may be held responsible for any wrong actions of your employees. This is due to the employees were technically under your watch.

37. a. To enhance the quality of your ongoing ethics analysis program, legal implications should be considered.

38. d. Although a business has the right to deny employees who are under 21 years of age from participating in pension plans, the rules may change if the underage employee has worked for the business for at least a year. The business can allow that person to participate in the pension plan, although this is at the employee's discretion.

39. b. A person must work for at least a year before they are eligible to participate in a pension plan.

40. d. The job description should include full information on what is expected from your workers. You need to inform recruits of the requirements of the job.

41. d. An employer has to ensure that the new hires are eligible to work in the United States.

42. d. Disparate treatment occurs when a person is treated differently due to being a part of a protected class. This is not to be confused with disparate impact, which occurs when a neutral employment action ends up causing harm.

43. b. When people do well at work and start to show positive results on their tests, a positive correlation can be noticed.

44. d. Corporate responsibility is being able to provide sensible assistance to the community.

45. a. Benchmarking is a consideration about how salaries are to be managed. Pay rates for internal jobs are to be matched to pay rates of jobs from outside the workplace.

46. d. The Worker Adjustment and Retraining Notification Act states that employers have to provide at least 60 days notice to people regarding any layoffs or closings. After this, the act may be applied to review terms for severance. Part of this includes providing the best severance offers to those who have more experience in the workplace.

47. d. A psychomotor test reviews how well a person is capable of managing certain tasks in the workplace based on physical functionality. This is different from a cognitive ability test that focuses on solving problems, or an aptitude test that focuses on general knowledge.

48. a. An exit interview helps you to determine the problems that are occurring in the workplace that precipitates an employee to be dissatisfied and quit.

49. a. An affirmative action plan should be installed in the workplace based on Executive Order 11246. Any company that has at least $10,000 in government contracts in a year cannot conduct discriminatory acts in the process of employment.

50. b. The Americans with Disabilities Act states that when considering employment you must ensure that you do not discriminate against people who have particular disabilities.

51. a. A behavioral question reviews the ways a person might be capable of managing certain tasks in the workplace. You can use a behavioral question to determine how a person is likely to engage in certain activities in the workplace.

52. d. The general needs assessment should consider how you're training people, but not necessarily conforming to any specific laws.

53. b. Content validity occurs when a person can confirm their ability to complete certain tasks. In this case, a person is able to pass a driving test.

54. c. A learning evaluation will determine if a person has been able to improve at work because of the training provided.

55. d. The USERRA rules state that a person who is called for active duty should be given employment credit for every month they serve in the military on active duty.

56. b. A needs assessment process is needed to develop new programs to allow for a line of succession in the workplace.

57. b. To get the answer, subtract the pre-test score from a post-test score and then divide by the pre-test score to determine the improvement. In this case, you would divide 10 by 50 to get 20%.

58. a. Opportunity bias occurs when the employee is given the praise or blame for a situation. This may occur in cases where the real cause is an action that was outside of their control at a time.

59. d. OSHA rules state that many things need to be provided to the workers for their protection and there are items that are not designated as essentials. Some things not covered in the OSHA rules include non-specialty forms of footwear, prescription-level items, and lifting belts among other items that may not be necessary or likely to be found in many working environments.

60. c. A hearing aid may be interpreted as something that would be used for personal needs and may not necessarily be used in all situations in the workplace. Therefore, you are under no obligation to provide coverage for this particular item.

61. c. A prosthetic is not a valid reason for accommodation.

62. c. The Foreign Corrupt Practices Act states that people cannot act improperly with international parties. Make payments to foreign government representatives is an improper business.

63. a. Any injuries that occur in the workplace must be recorded according to OSHA standards provided that the place of business employees at least ten people.

64. d. Because the company has fewer than ten employees, the company does not have to comply with OSHA rules.

65. c. The key is to note if the injury in question is substantial and would require the worker to miss a lot of time at work due to the issue.

Conclusion

Consider your human resources knowledge before taking the SHRM-CP or SCP tests. The process for taking the test may seem simple, but the extensive body of knowledge you will need will be a challenge in its own right.

You can use the exams in this guide to help you identify what you might be questioned on the tests. You will find that the tests in this guide are very effective to gage your knowledge in the field and how well you understand the concepts introduced.

Good luck with your efforts.

Made in the USA
San Bernardino, CA
17 May 2019